L. T. Paddock
Bouldeo
Colo

Mr. and Mrs.
Laurence T. Paddock
525 - 13th St.
Boulder, Colorado 80302

NEW FRONTIER

NEW FRONTIER
SAGA OF THE NORTH FORK
BY WILSON ROCKWELL

ILLUSTRATIONS BY
JOSEPHINE McKITTRICK

THE WORLD PRESS, INC.
DENVER, COLORADO
1938

Printed in the United States of America

BY THE WORLD PRESS, INC.
1837 Champa Street
Denver, Colo.

CONTENTS

CONTENTS

A LAST TRIBUTE

A LAST TRIBUTE

In 1908 a young bride, who looked much younger than her twenty-three years, came from the East to make her home in the North Fork. She had recently attended an exclusive eastern women's college and was one of the most popular belles in the wealthy city of Bradford, Pennsylvania.

She turned her back on the social life, luxuries, and advantages to which she was accustomed to begin a new life with her husband on Colorado's last frontier. The slender girl soon won the hearts of the rough but sincere pioneers of the North Fork. Her friendliness, unselfishness, and kindness became a local tradition. No one was ever turned from her door empty-handed. The humblest North Fork unfortunate knew that he could always find a hospitable reception at her home. Children made a habit of stopping there to sell magazines, newspapers, tickets, vegetables, and other commodities, for they always found a ready customer in the gracious lady who lived in the green and white house on the corner of Third Street. Her sympathetic soul responded to every case of need, and her numerous Christmas and charitable gifts brought happiness to many an underprivileged family.

Typical of her daily acts of service was the time she sat up all night with an unconscious neighbor boy who had been injured in an automobile accident. While living on her husband's cattle ranch at Maher, she saddled her horse late one night and rode several miles to assist at the birth of a baby in a nearby cow-camp. The baby proved to be a girl and was named after the young easterner who helped usher her into the world.

When the wife of an aged Paonia neighbor died a few years ago, the heart-broken old man found his greatest comfort in the genuine sympathy that was given him by this cosmopolitan woman, who invariably put the welfare of others before that of herself. One of the finest tributes ever paid a woman came from this old man when he wrote, "I will always remember her as the most beautiful and kindliest person I have ever known."

Her life was centered around her family, and she never spoke a cross or unkind word to any of its members. In her husband's service of two terms as state representative, one term as state senator, and one term as lieutenant governor, she graciously acceded to the inconvenient demands of public life, devoting herself to his welfare even to accompanying him almost invariably on his frequent journeys. In his long campaign as Republican candidate for governor of Colorado she went with him at the suggestion of Republican leaders that she was the best vote-getter in the state. When later he was appointed to the State Board of Agriculture by a Democratic governor, she continued the custom as he traveled monthly or oftener to official duty at the Colorado State College in Fort Collins and at its branches and field stations throughout the state.[1]

Whenever she visited the East, the cultured circle of her youth welcomed her with open arms. Countless parties at fashionable country clubs and in stately homes were held in her honor. Her eastern friends flocked around her then as they had before she was married, anxious to again see the charming personality around which conversations seemed to gravitate. She was one of those rare individuals who is equally at home in a drawing room or in a cow-camp, and she had the unusual distinction of being adored by people of all classes.

Thirty years after she had established her home in the North Fork, she left on a trip with her husband, destined never to return again. However, the spirit of this kindly character is an integral part of the North Fork tradition and will never be forgotten. While reared in a different environment, she loved this country and its people, and they in turn loved her.

Each Christmas, for several years, she and her husband sent as their greeting novel monthly calendars bearing inspirational verses and other quotations. Peculiarly enough, the dominant lines on the page for March, 1938, the month she so unexpectedly died, are singularly applicable to her:

[1] Craig, A. L., "Multitudes Grieve as Death Ends Career of Widely Beloved Woman," *The Paonian,* March 10, 1938.

They are not dead who live
In lives they leave behind;
In those whom they have blessed
They live a life again
And shall live through the years,
Eternal life, and grow
Each day more beautiful
As time declares their good
. . . and proves
Their immortality.[2]

This book is dedicated as a last tribute to that eastern girl who became a westerner and left a memory in the North Fork which will never die. She was Aileen Miller Rockwell, my mother.

[2] Craig, A. L., "She Lives Again," *The Paonian,* March 10, 1938.

Aileen Rockwell in 1908

PREFACE

PREFACE

THE North Fork country, a small area in the west central portion of Colorado, lies within parts of Delta, Montrose, and Gunnison counties. This picturesque, mountainous land is drained by the North Fork, from which stream the region derives its name, the Smith Fork, and Crystal Creek tributaries to the Gunnison River, most famous fishing stream of the West. Roughly speaking, the North Fork country is bounded on the north by Grand Mesa, on the south by Black Mesa, on the west by the Black Canyon of the Gunnison River, and on the east by the Elk Mountains.

This little known section of the Rocky Mountains has had a romantic and varied history, but because it is situated so far off the beaten path, its illustrious and unusual past has not been preserved. Since life is always interesting, whether found in sophisticated, man-made metropolises, or amid the simpler but more resplendent beauties of nature, I have tried to picture a little of this colorful country's story before it is forever lost in the silent graves of its few remaining pioneers.

However, the primary motive for writing this book is personal. To me the North Fork country reflects the cherished memories of childhood, youth, and home.

I grew up in this seclusive portion of Colorado and had the privilege of knowing well some of the personalities appearing in this narrative. Most of the characters who live on the stage of this story have passed on, and it will not be long before the remaining few follow. Nevertheless, the impressions they have made for themselves in this part of the state will remain immortal so long as there is anyone left to remember and appreciate. The purpose of this work, therefore, is to rekindle and prolong the memory and appreciation for the early North Fork and its pioneers by resurrecting a nearly buried past and making it live again.

Some of the selections included in this book were published in various magazines and newspapers throughout the state, and I wish to express my appreciation to the following editors and publishers for their permission to reprint said selections and their release of publication rights and copyrights to me: Dr. L. R. Hafen of the *Colorado Magazine*, Dr. L. J. Davidson of *Space*, A. L. Craig of *The Paonian*, B. H. Lyle of *The Hotchkiss Herald*, and A. R. Knight of *The Crawford Chronicle*.

INTRODUCTION

I
THE WHITE TIDE

THE WHITE TIDE

FOR centuries Colorado remained in the undisturbed possession of the redskins, who fought, loved, hunted, and died on its wild plains and mountains. Then, in 1765, the first gentle lapping of the approaching great tide of the white race became audible to the Colorado denizens. During that year Governor Cachupin of New Mexico, then a part of Spanish territory, sent an expedition to explore the unknown northern lands. Don Juan Rivera led this group into southwestern Colorado and north to the Uncompahgre River which the Spaniards followed to its junction with the Gunnison at the present site of Delta. While camped there Rivera carved a cross on a cottonwood tree as a landmark for future travelers. Escalante refers to this cross in his journal:

Farther down the river [the Uncompahgre] and about four leagues north of this plain of San Augustine the river forms a junction with a larger one, called by the people of our party the River of San Javier [Gunnison] and by the Yutas [Ute Indians] the River Tomichi. There came to these two rivers in the year 1765 Don Juan Maria de Rivera. . . The place where he camped before crossing the river [Uncompahgre] and where he said he cut the figure of a cross on a young poplar tree, with the initials of his name and the year of his expedition, are still found at the junction of these rivers on the southern bank, as we were informed by our interpreter.[1]

[1] W. R. Harris, *The Catholic Church in Utah (1776-1909)*, p. 146.

Other early Spanish explorations followed Rivera's general route and journeyed near the North Fork section to spread the gospel, pursue runaway slaves, punish marauders, and trade with the Indians. However, it was not until eleven years after Rivera's expedition that the first white men entered the North Fork. In 1776, a few months after the thirteen American colonies had drawn up and signed the Declaration of Independence, a small party of twelve men, led by Fathers Escalante and Dominguez, started out to find an inland route from Santa Fe, New Mexico, to the Spanish missions which Junipero Serra had established in Monterey, California.

Escalante and Dominguez made their way into southern Colorado near the present location of Pagosa Springs. In order to avoid the high mountains to the north, they pursued a westerly course through what is now the city of Durango to the Dolores River. They were forced to ford many rivers between Pagosa Springs and the Dolores River, including the Piedra,[2] Los Pinos,[3] Florida,[4] Animas,[5] and the Mancos.[6] Escalante and Dominguez named many of these rivers.

[2] Harris, p. 130. ". . . and a league farther on we arrived at another river called the Piedra at a point near its junction with the Navajo."

[3] *Ibid.*, p. 131. "Crossing the river [the Piedra] we traveled two leagues to the west and a little more than two to the west-northwest and arrived at the eastern bank of the river . . . the Rio de los Pinos (Pine River) because of the pine trees growing on its banks."

[4] *Ibid.* "We left the river Pinos . . . and . . . arrived at the River Florida which is much smaller. . ."

[5] *Ibid.* "Passing the River Florida we . . . came to the River de las Animas. . ."

[6] *Ibid.*, p. 133. "We left the River Animas (River of Souls) . . . and were obliged to stop by the first of two small streams which make up the San Lozaro, otherwise called Las Mancos."

The two friars then followed the Dolores River[7] through the Disappointment country as far north as Naturita. The roughness of the country near Bedrock[8] forced them eastward to the San Miguel River[9] down which they traveled in a southeasterly direction to a point near Placerville.

Crossing the Dallas Divide between Placerville and Ridgeway, the famous explorers proceeded down into the valley of the Uncompahgre,[10] a Ute word meaning Colorado (red lake).[11] Once more they turned northwest along the banks of the Uncompahgre River to again continue towards their destination on the West Coast—over a thousand miles away. Near present Montrose they unexpectedly met a Ute warrior and his family.[12] After a brief visit with the Indian

[7] *Ibid.* "We passed through a piece of burnt-over woodland with scant pasturage and turned to the north, crossing the Rio de Neustra Senora de los Dolores (River of our Lady of Sorrows)."

[8] *Ibid.*, p. 137. "Two of our companions left very early to find when we could best leave the river [Dolores], for here the banks are very high and stony. . . In the bed of the river there are quantities of rocks, and we feared to injure the horses, having to cross it several times."

Ibid., pp. 137-140. "Wishing to cross the ridge of high and rocky table lands, for the river bed now became impassable, one of the men went on ahead to see if the road was passable. He found that we could not travel the northwest road but discovered another path to the southeast . . . we came to the Rio San Pedro [San Miguel] . . . which runs toward the north, turns to the northwest, and then to the west until it unites with the Dolores."

[10] Harris, *Op. Cit.*, p. 143. "We now began to cross the mountains in a northeasterly direction. . . We finished the descent of the mountain and entered the pleasant valley of the river of San Francisco [Uncompahgre]."

[11] *Ibid.*, ". . . called by the Yutas the Ancapogari, which the interpreter tells us means Colorado Lake, from the fact that near its source there is a spring of reddish water, hot and disagreeable to the taste."

[12] *Ibid.*, "We left the San Francisco mountain and journeyed down the river in a northwesterly direction; and having traveled a short distance we met a Yuta [Ute] by the name of Surdo with his family."

by means of an interpreter the friars continued northeast to the Gunnison below where it is joined by the North Fork. Escalante describes this course in his journal:

> We left the plain of San Augustine, leaving the river of San Francisco [Uncompahgre] to the north and traveled half a league [1 league equals 2.63 miles], going three leagues and a half to the northeast on good ground and without stones and arrived at the San Javier [Gunnison] . . . We then proceeded up the river until we came to some villages.[13]

From here two of the Spaniards were sent to procure guides while the others put up camp to await results. The next morning five Utes appeared on the opposite side of the North Fork to talk with the Spaniards. Escalante describes the event:

> We gave them something to eat and to smoke but after a long conversation about the difficulties they had had during the summer with the Comanches we could not get from them anything useful to our interests because their design was to make us afraid, exaggerating the danger to which we were exposing ourselves, as the Comanches would kill us if we continued on this course. We destroyed the force of the pretexts with which they tried to stop our progress by saying to them that our God, who is above all, would defend us in case of an encounter with our enemies.[14]

On the following day the interpreters and guide arrived with five Indians. These Utes also attempted to persuade the Spaniards to discontinue their journey and turn back or be massacred by the Comanches. However, after much effort, guides were finally se-

[13] *Ibid.*, p. 146.
[14] *Ibid.*, p. 147.

cured. Instead of escorting the Spaniards back to the Gunnison and continuing westward as they should have done, the guides, probably trying to deceive the Spaniards, went northeast, following the North Fork to where Leroux Creek joins it a short distance below the present town of Hotchkiss. At this junction the Indians, apparently believing that further deception might be dangerous, turned up the creek and led the party over Grand Mesa, picturesque home of a hundred lakes and the largest flat-topped mountain in the world. From this mesa the group advanced to the Colorado River near where the town of De Beque now stands, continuing northwestward to Utah Lake. This was as far west as the explorers reached. Escalante gives the reasons for not continuing on:

The winter had now set in with great rigor [October] and all the mountain ranges that we could see were covered with snow; the weather was very changeable and long before we could reach [Monterey] the mountain passes would be closed up... The provisions we had brought were now nearly exhausted, and if we continued to go on we would be liable to perish with hunger if not with cold.[15]

From here the Spaniards journeyed south through Utah and arrived in Santa Fe January 2, 1777. Although Escalante and Dominguez did not find an inland route to Monterey, they journeyed over 1300 miles on foot and unarmed to complete a trip which, though it failed in its objective, was a remarkable feat of stamina and courage.

[15] Harris, *Op. Cit.*, p. 192-193.

Even before the white and red races had begun their inevitable struggle in the Colorado mountains and valleys, the Indians resented the appearance of the advance guard of white explorers. Perhaps the Colorado aborigines sensed already at this early date the meaning and future results of the rising tide of their approaching conquerors. At any rate, it was only because of Indian trickery that Escalante, Dominguez, and their band of Spanish pathfinders entered the North Fork country, the first white pioneers to journey through this untamed home of the Utes. With the arrival of these newcomers the North Fork, as well as the rest of Colorado, became a part of the Spanish dominion. This expedition ranked as the most outstanding exploration of western Colorado until the coming of Captain Gunnison in 1853.

Over fifty years passed before the ebbing white tide once more began rising into the lofty mountains of western Colorado. During the late eighteen-thirties, Antoine Robidoux, a French trader from St. Louis, set up a fur trading post just below the confluence of the Uncompahgre and Gunnison rivers near the present site of Delta. This log fort served as a general outfitting and trading center for those who came to hunt and trap in the wilds of the Uncompahgre and North Fork countries. However, the new trading post was shortlived, for soon after its establishment, the Utes set fire to the log buildings, and again the white tide was temporarily checked. Captain Gunnison noted the ruins of the old trading fort when he passed

it during his memorable expedition fifty years later.[16]
Lieutenant Beckwith, a member of Gunnison's party,
recorded:

> We crossed the point of land lying between the Uncompahgre
> and Grand [Gunnison] [17] rivers reaching the latter at Roubi-
> deau's [Robidoux] old trading fort, now entirely fallen to ruins.[18]

The United States government claimed all the land
within the present boundaries of Colorado as American territory by 1848 although the Indians refused to
recognize it. When the Louisiana Purchase was made
from Napoleon in 1803 that portion of eastern Colorado drained by the Platte and Arkansas rivers passed
to the United States. During the second decade of the
nineteenth century Mexico won its independence
from Spain and acquired the greater portion of the
large Spanish dominion in North America, which included western and southeastern Colorado. The southeastern corner between the Arkansas and the Rio
Grande rivers was Mexican territory from 1819 to
1836 when Texas broke away from Mexico. In 1845
this section of Colorado came into the Union as part
of the state of Texas although it continued to be
claimed by Mexico until the conclusion of the Mexican War in 1848. In 1850 it became a part of the
public domain by virtue of a boundary agreement
between Texas and the federal government. Western
Colorado, including the North Fork, remained under

[16] September 17, 1853.
[17] The Grand River is now called the Colorado. However, in this instance Lieutenant Beckwith meant the Gunnison.
[18] Beckwith, *Reports of Explorations and Surveys,* Volume II, 1855, p. 56.

the parental care of Mexico until it was ceded to the
United States on February 2, 1848, by the treaty of
Guadalupe Hidalgo, which ended this nation's war
with Mexico. Consequently, Colorado has paid alleg-
iance to five different flags—the flag of Spain, of
France, of Mexico, of Texas, and of the United States.

Although by this time Colorado had become a part
of the United States, the region was not quickly settled.[19] The primary reason for this delay was due to
the general misconception that the Rocky Mountain
country was unfit for settlement. Major Stephen H.
Long, who was sent in 1819 by John C. Calhoun, then
Secretary of War, to explore the country north of the
Spanish possessions above the Arkansas River, started
this belief because of his mistaken impression of the
region:

> In regard to this extensive section of country we do not hesi-
> tate in giving the opinion that it is almost wholly unfit for culti-
> vation and, of course, uninhabitable by a people depending upon
> agriculture for their subsistence. Although tracts of fertile land,
> considerably extensive, are occasionally to be met with, yet the
> scarcity of wood and water, almost uniformly prevalent, will
> prove an insuperable obstacle in the way of settling the country.
> . . . The whole of this region seems peculiarly adapted as a range
> for buffalo, wild goats, and other wild game, incalculable multi-
> tudes of which find ample pasturage and subsistence upon it.
>
> This region, however, viewed as a frontier may prove of infinite
> importance to the United States, inasmuch as it is calculated to
> serve as a barrier to prevent too great an extension of our popula-
> tion westward and secure us against the machinations of excur-

---

[19] It was not until 1861 that Congress passed an act establishing Colorado as a territory. This act was signed by Abraham Lincoln. A census
taken at that time stated that there were 20,798 male whites, 4,484 female
whites, and 89 negroes. Colorado did not become a state until 1876.

sions of an enemy that might otherwise be disposed to annoy us in that part of our frontier.[20]

It was not until 1853 that there was any exploration in western Colorado which rivaled the one made by Fathers Escalante and Dominguez seventy-seven years before. During that year Captain John W. Gunnison of the Topographical Engineers was sent by the Secretary of War, Jefferson Davis, to survey a route for a transcontinental railroad across the Rockies. Although Captain Gunnison never trod upon North Fork soil, he circled within a short distance of it.

Near Sapinero, about twenty-six miles west of Gunnison, the Gunnison River starts flowing through a narrow high canyon, in places measuring over 2000 feet in depth.[21] Unable to go through this picturesque cut, which forms the western boundary of the North Fork country, Captain Gunnison led his party of engineers over Blue Mesa, which extends around the southern and western sides of the black-appearing gorge to the site of the present state bridge, ten miles above Delta, where the canyon ends. At this point Captain Gunnison forded the river which today bears his name in honor of his memorable expedition. Lieutenant Beckwith's report mentions their excursion around what is now known as Black Canyon:

[20] *Account of an Expedition from Pittsburgh to the Rocky Mountains under Command of Major S. H. Long,* Compiled by Edwin James from notes of Major Long, Volume II, p. 361.

[21] The Black Canyon of the Gunnison measures from 1,725 feet to 2,240 feet in depth and 1,000 to 3,000 feet in width.

The canyon [Black Canyon] which we have been so many days passing around terminates several [10] miles above the junction of the Uncompahgre with the Grand River [Gunnison River].[22]

The North Fork was long the favorite hunting ground of the Utes. In the summer they hunted and fished in the mountains and valleys of this rugged country, and during the winter months they camped on the plains below, near Delta and Montrose. The Utes were true children of the mountains, and John V. Plake, part Indian, tells in colorful Indian style why this was so according to an old tradition among the Tabbequache, one of the Ute tribes which roamed the North Fork:

Once in the long ago the god, Keeche Manitou, rewarding the brave, had given them [the Utes] the mountains with their crystal streams and sheltered valleys, leaving only the parched plains and roving herds of buffalo to the vanquished [the plains Indians]. In the foothills where plain and mountain meet the Ute braves defied their enemies, [of the plains] the Algonquins, Cheyennes, and Arapahoes. When pressed in battle the canyons and gorges had furnished the Ute braves with strongholds and their enemies had been kept from gaining any of the territory west of the Divide.[23]

A note of pathos creeps into his words as the author gives an account of the rapidly rising white tide which had continued to ebb and flow, gradually getting higher and higher, sweeping away the plains In-

[22] Again Lieutenant Beckwith mistakenly refers to the Gunnison as the Grand River, *Op. Cit.,* p. 56.

[23] John V. Plake, "The Exodus of the Utes," original manuscript, 1922. In possession of the State Historical Society of Colorado.

Black Canyon of the Gunnison River

dians and pressing slowly but persistently upward
along the seemingly impregnable Colorado mountains:

> But now the white men had come to claim it [the mountains]
> as a birthright of the strong. The Utes, seeing how quickly the
> Cheyennes and their allies were subdued and fearing that they too
> might be forced on to reservations, were finally willing to relin-
> quish to the whites a large portion of their mountain country in
> order to gain their friendship. So, when Kit Carson and the terri-
> torial governor urged the treaty [of 1868] upon them they did
> not demur. They understood it as a measure for their own pro-
> tection which would guarantee them against any further en-
> croachment of the paleface. It was in the hills of Cochetopa,
> in 1868, that the Uncompahgres accepted supervision of the
> white man's government.[24]

The treaty of 1868[25] pushed the Utes over the Con-
tinental Divide into far western Colorado. Two agencies were established here, one near White River in
northern Colorado and the other on Los Pinos Creek
near Gunnison. When gold was found in the San Juan
Mountains, the Los Pinos agency was moved, by the
treaty of 1873,[26] farther west to the Uncompahgre,
of which the North Fork country was a part. While
those who drew up and signed these treaties probably
thought that they would last, the indomitable advancing movement of gold seekers, pioneers, and settlers could not be stopped.

Friction soon resulted between the two races, as
prospectors, hunters, and homeseekers trickled into the
reservations. The Indian agents also contributed to

[24] Plake, *Op. Cit.*
[25] See Appendix for contents of treaty.
[26] See Appendix for contents of treaty.

this ill-feeling since they were often incompetent, dishonest, or failed to understand Indian character. Nathan C. Meeker, White River agent, was one of this latter type. Meeker was determined to civilize and Christianize the Utes at once. He refused to let them go on their accustomed hunting trips and tried to make them over night into competent farmers, cutting off rations as a penalty for their refusal to work.

Conflict was inevitable. The White River Utes made a feeble but desperate last stand against the irresistible tide which had driven them against their final stronghold at the end of the trail. Two subchiefs, Douglas and Jack, were leaders of the savages who massacred twelve men and kidnapped three women at the Meeker Agency in 1879. The two warlike chiefs also led their band against three companies of cavalry which were marching toward the reservation from Rawlins, Wyoming, in response to reports that trouble was brewing on White River. At Milk Creek, twenty-five miles from the agency, the Indians surrounded the little group and held them in siege for six days until word was received from Chief Ouray to stop fighting. Forty-seven soldiers were wounded and thirteen killed, including the commander, Major Thomas T. Thornburg.

Ouray, head chief of the Utes, was living at the time of the Meeker Massacre on the Uncompahgre River near the present city of Montrose. This unusual man and his equally remarkable wife, Chipeta, realized the futility of warring against the white tide, and

Chief Ouray

—*Courtesy The Paonian*

they were largely responsible for checking the war-like temperament of their restless and fierce race, which was being cornered and caged like wild animals.

When Ouray was informed of the massacre and the Milk Creek encounter, he immediately sent orders to cease fighting. Chipeta rode on horseback from the Uncompahgre to Douglas's camp on the Colorado River and rescued the three women captives, the living victims of a great tragedy of western history. John V. Plake in his "Exodus of the Utes" comments on the episode:

How then shall we of this later day, having knowledge of the injustices inflicted upon them [the Indians], place all the blame upon the Utes for the horrible massacre that occurred on White River in September, 1879? But there were innocent ones among those whom the Indians slaughtered. Aye, and there were innocent ones, helpless old men, women, and children among the Cheyennes who were slaughtered at Sand Creek in 1864 in eastern Colorado under the leadership of Chivington, an officer of the Government. Some historians have made a distinction, where none exists, when they name the one as a horrible massacre by blood-thirsty savages and the other as a glorious victory for civilized men.[27]

The Meeker Massacre hastened the inevitable exodus of the Uncompahgre and White River Utes to the Uintah reservation in Utah.[28] By act of Congress they were removed from the North Fork region, part of the Uncompahgre reservation, in September, 1881, and the territory was thrown open for settlement.

[27] Plake, *Op. Cit.*
[28] See Appendix for the treaty of 1880.

Thus, although no individual Ute was punished for the White River uprising, the entire tribe was made to suffer. Chief Ouray died with a broken heart the year his crestfallen people were ordered to leave forever their beloved Colorado. The White Tide had finally conquered.

PART I
TAMING THE WILDERNESS

II
INDIAN WELCOME

INDIAN WELCOME

SHORTLY after the deplorable events at the White River Agency in northern Colorado, word spread that the Uncompahgre and White River Utes would be removed from their reservations and the region thrown open to settlers. This news was of special interest to men of pioneer blood, those restless and hardy forerunners of settlement who led the westward movement across the United States until they had become hemmed in by their greatest foe—civilization. With the opening of a new virgin country some of these pioneers again had the opportunity to lead the way over mysterious and intriguing divides to conquer another unsettled wilderness. Even before the Utes were taken away, a few of these pathfinders braved the dangers of unfriendly Indians to explore this little-known land and "spot" their claims.

As early as 1879, two years before the final exodus of the former rulers of Colorado, Enos Hotchkiss, discoverer of the well known Golden Fleece mine at Lake City and toll road partner of Otto Mears—the Pathfinder of the San Juan, learned from the agent at Fort Crawford, the Uncompahgre cantonment, that the Indian country would be opened for settlement as soon as a treaty could be made with the Utes.

In August, Hotchkiss set out from Lake City for the Uncompahgre reservation, of which the North Fork was a part. He rode a mare with a colt to mislead the Indians into believing that she was a stray, in case they should notice her tracks. He had not progressed far in Indian territory when he saw a group of horsemen in the distance. From their style of riding he immediately recognized them as Indians, and apparently they had seen him, for they were moving in his direction. He took a firm grip on his rifle and waited, familiar enough with Indian character to know that flight would make even more hazardous his chance of escape.

Their stolid faces gave no sign of his fate as they approached somewhat warily. Suddenly a big buck kicked his horse and galloped toward him. Hotchkiss was startled at this unexpected onslaught and steeled himself for an emergency.

"How!" grunted the Indian as he neared, raising his arm in a friendly gesture. For the first time Hotchkiss recognized the warrior as Indian Charlie, nephew of the head chief of all the Utes—the famous Chief Ouray. With a feeling of relief the white man remembered that several years before he had saved Indian Charlie's life when the latter had been attacked by three drunken frontiersmen on the Saguache-Lake City toll road.

"Where go?" queried the Ute as he pulled his buckskin pony to a stop.

"Hunting horses," lied Hotchkiss.

"Go ahead. No see you," the chief said with a faint smile, motioning for his hostile looking companions to follow him as he rode away. Indian Charlie had paid his debt.

Hotchkiss spent a month on the reservation, riding and camping on the mesas to avoid the Indians who had become warlike in their bitterness against the whites, who were seeking to drive them from their last hold on the home and hunting grounds of their ancestors.

The white scout entered the North Fork country through the now almost extinct shimmering white sage of Rogers Mesa—worthy gateway to a colorful land. When he reached the end of the mesa, he dismounted and gazed for the first time at the valley below. Through his spy glass he located two Indian villages, one at the present site of Paonia and the other a few miles farther down the valley on Angevine Creek. A small clearing in the oak brush at the foot of the mesa particularly attracted his attention. It was a fertile piece of land within easy reach of water on which the Indians raised corn. Much deer hair, used by squaws in tanning hides, lay on the ground, evidencing a recent Indian camp.

Striding over to the suckling colt, Hotchkiss patted him on the back. "Condimit!" he said, using his favorite expletive. "We've come a long way to find it, but some day that old corn field down there will be our home."

Due to his long absence Hotchkiss's family had given him up as lost or killed by the Indians. One afternoon they saw him come riding home in the opposite direction from which he had left, having made a complete circle of the Uncompahgre Indian country to make a "strike" which brought him as much satisfaction as his prior discovery of the rich Golden Fleece mine—the finding of an Indian corn field in the North Fork Valley.

A few other adventuresome pioneers were also willing to risk the loss of their scalps in order to line up their claims before the North Fork country was officially opened for settlement. This gave them an opportunity to discover choice plots of land which could be staked out as soon as the Utes were removed and the rush started.

With this objective, six prospective settlers rode on to the reservation. They set up their camp along the North Fork River a short distance below Rogers Mesa. On the following morning the party split up to explore the country, three of the group riding up on the mesa while Henry Roberts, Bill Meredith, and Jay Smith remained in the valley.

While Roberts was looking over the upper part of the valley, he noticed some sort of Indian trinket lying on the ground near Angevine Creek. He swung from his horse to examine the object more closely. He was leaning over to pick it up when two Indian horsemen suddenly appeared out of the oak brush and came charging down on him at top speed. At this unexpected assault Roberts's colt reared and broke away, leaving his rider with no means of escape.

Enos Hotchkiss

"Hi, Hi!" Roberts cried, waving his arm in friendly salutation at the approaching Utes. However, the warriors paid no heed to his greetings and continued to gallop toward him.

Again Roberts shouted at the Indians, but this time he covered them with his Winchester. At sight of the rifle the Indians slowed down their ponies and showed a willingness to talk.

One of them pointed at the sun and said, "All pale-faces must be off Indian land before see sun tomorrow or they die." Without further discussion they turned their horses and rode away. Roberts hastened back to camp and informed his two companions of the warning.

"That's all I want to know," commented Meredith. "I'm hittin' the trail as soon as I can get my horses packed."

Roberts and Smith waited until sundown before following, leaving a note at the camp to inform the others of the threat. It gradually grew dark as they jogged along on the Old Indian Trail, the Ute highway which extended from the North Fork country over Black Mesa through the site of present-day Gunnison and wound southward as far as Saguache in the San Luis Valley. This trail was the main thoroughfare into the North Fork and was usually followed by the early explorers and settlers except when they came by wagon. It later became known as the Old Hartman Trail due to Sam Hartman's use of it for driving cattle.

The two men were following this narrow, beaten path through the present location of Crawford when Smith's horse suddenly snorted and came to a stop, peering with pricked ears into the darkness, accentuated by a clump of cedars directly ahead.

"Come on! What's the trouble?" Smith exclaimed, jingling his spurs on the bronco's sides. The horse reared and jumped to the side.

"Those cedars seem to have him spooked," observed Roberts. "Let's go around 'em." Circling the trees they crossed the Smith Fork of the Gunnison and again entered the trail.

"Look back!" ejaculated Roberts softly.

Smith turned in his saddle. A small fire was flickering at the top of the hill behind them. "That looks like a signal," whispered Smith. "They're sure keepin' an eye on us."

"Say, are those Indians coming out of those cedars up along the trail?"

"By God, I believe so. No wonder your horse wouldn't go in there. Let's get the hell out o' here!"

Throughout the night other signal fires flashed from various points, marking the white men's progress out of the country. The next morning the tired, dusty riders met Enos Hotchkiss and the Duke brothers who were camped on Black Mesa with a herd of horses.

"I saw your partner last evening," Enos remarked to the fugitives, "and he seemed to be in a hurry."

"So are we," Smith answered. "The Ute reception committee gave us a real Indian welcome."

III
FRONTIER JUSTICE

FRONTIER JUSTICE

WHEN the Uncompahgre reservation was opened for settlement in September, 1881, long lines of wagons streamed into the region. Settlers entered the North Fork section chiefly by way of Black Mesa, the leaders forming the resemblance of a wagon road which the others followed. Enos Hotchkiss and George and Will Duke were among the first to drive their teams into the virgin land, staking out their pre-emption claims near the present site of Hotchkiss.

As soon as Will Duke had made his claim, he drove up on the Poison Springs range, thirteen miles southwest of Crawford, to look after a herd of horses which had been turned there several days before. He had not been there long when he received word that another settler had jumped his claim. Hitching up his ox-team, he started back to defend his property.

Will's oxen were fording the North Fork near where the town of Hotchkiss now stands when an armed man suddenly stepped out from the brush along the river bank. Pointing his rifle at the teamster, he remarked, "It looks like I've got your ranch."

Will grinned, glancing back at his gun which lay in the wagon just out of reach. "Well, I guess we can fix it up all right," he said pleasantly as he neared the shore. Without further comment the gunman turned and disappeared in the brush.

The next morning Will, accompanied by his brother, George, and Dave Platt, began the construction of a cabin on the disputed tract. They completed the foundations before noon, but while they were away eating dinner at Hotchkiss's cabin, the claim-jumper tore down the logs.

When the three builders again arrived on the scene, they looked with dismay at the destruction of their morning's work. "I've gotta see this fellow," Will said, "and one of us is definitely goin' to own this place before sundown."

Mounting their horses the three men rode down the valley a short distance and approached a tent where several men were camped. Platt rode a little behind his two companions, and before they reached the tent, he dismounted and levelled his Winchester over the cantle of his saddle. There were several men lounging by the tent, and Will immediately recognized one of them as his rival.

"So you didn't like my cabin?" he questioned, swinging down from his horse.

"Not when it's on my land," replied the other, looking with uneasiness into the barrel of Platt's rifle.

"No gun play is necessary," said George as one of the men reached for his six-shooter. "The only legal way to settle this matter is to make a circle in that little clearing down yonder by them cottonwood trees and let the contestants fight it out, the winner takin' the ranch."

"But he's bigger than me," observed the defendant.

"That can't be helped now," George replied.

"It'll take me about fifteen minutes to go over there and make that ring," said Will, "and if you're still here when I get back, we'll go on trial with our fists."

Will returned from the clearing just in time to see the claim-jumper and his friends drive hurriedly away in a small two-wheeled cart on which they had speedily piled their camping outfit. The pioneer court had rendered its verdict.

The following fall Enos Hotchkiss and the two young Duke brothers, George and Will, drove to Cebolla Creek for supplies, leaving Dave Platt in charge of their North Fork holdings. At Gunnison they loaded three wagons with provisions and started back. They struck a blizzard on Black Mesa which delayed them several days. However, they finally reached their destination after an absence of more than two weeks —only to find a most unfriendly welcome awaiting them.

Platt gazed at them suspiciously when they drove up. "You're Masons, ain't yuh?" he questioned, leveling his gun at them.

"Don't yuh remember us, Dave?" Hotchkiss asked, somewhat surprised at the reception.

Platt curled his lip viciously. "You Masons have

come to kill me, but you're not gonna get the chance."

The newcomers soon realized that Platt had lost his mind during his lonely sojourn, and they finally managed to get his gun away from him before he did any damage.

A weird sight greeted their eyes when they entered the cabin. A keg of syrup had been poured out into the middle of the floor and stirred up with dried cherries and a chest of tea. Numerous sacks of flour were piled up against the door, some of which had been slit open, scattering flour in all directions. Platt had also killed the dogs and buried them underneath the floor.

"I killed 'em because they went mad," he explained.

"Probably starving to death," suggested Hotchkiss to George.

"He's crazier than a loon," whispered George. "What are we goin' to do with 'im?"

A hole had been torn out of the top of the cabin, and Platt had spent the greater part of each day sitting on the roof with his rifle, guarding the cabin against imaginary foes. While at his post he had shot a deer, which had been his only food supply since he had destroyed his other provisions ten days before the arrival of his employers.

On the smooth-planed door of the cabin the madman had kept a record of each day's peculiar actions. Among other monstrosities was an account of his tying his only horse in the timber without feed or water. Upon investigation George discovered the gaunt victim nearly dead of starvation and thirst. Replacing the rope that she had nearly twisted off, George led her down to the river to drink.

After watering the mare he started to tie her behind one of the wagons when Platt, who had recovered and loaded his gun, without warning shot the horse through the head. As Platt began reloading, George ran for a nearby tree.

"You ain't got no sand!" Platt laughed, slipping another cartridge into the barrel. Hotchkiss, seeing the danger, ran up from behind, hit Platt over the head, and recaptured the rifle. After this experience the lunatic acquiesced to everything Hotchkiss ordered of him.

"Go ahead and eat your meal," Hotchkiss said to the sullen man that evening when he refused to touch his supper.

"It's poisoned," responded Platt, furtively eying Hotchkiss, "but if I have to eat it, I will."

After supper Hotchkiss told Platt to fiddle for them, and much to everyone's surprise he could play as well as ever, his insanity having no effect on his skill with the fiddle.

A few days later Hotchkiss paid Platt his wages and asked a transient employee to escort him as far as Gunnison, the nearest railroad station, and buy him a ticket for his home in Missouri. Several years later Hotchkiss received a letter from Platt's sister inquiring about her brother. Apparently their unfortunate friend had never arrived home.

"I wonder if he ever caught his train," Will remarked after he had finished reading the letter.

"That's something we'll never know," replied Hotchkiss, "but anything might have happened between two men in a wilderness—especially when one of them was a madman with a payroll."

IV
VIRGIN SOIL

VIRGIN SOIL

FIFTY-SIX years have passed since the first wagon made its slow and laborious way up the North Fork Valley from Hotchkiss to Paonia.[1] Through sagebrush, soft ground, and treacherous creeks it picked its course, accompanied by the first pioneers to establish their claims and blaze the trail into the great fruit region of Colorado. Since then these pathfinders have crossed over another Great Divide to explore other unknown valleys, but North Fork residents will never forget them and their distinguished leader, Samuel Wade, founder of Paonia.

Samuel Wade, Indian fighter and Civil War captain, examined the Uncompahgre reservation soon after it was opened for settlement and finally located the plot of land where he later made his claim, believing it to be in one of the most fertile sections of the valley. A short time later he made his second trip over in company with his brother Joseph, his son Ezra, Sam Angevine, Doug McIntyre, George Root, William Clarke, and Enos Hotchkiss. The names of all these men are closely associated with the early life and development of this new frontier.

Carrying about four hundred pounds of supplies

[1] September, 1881.

in their two wagons, they left the wagon road which extended to Curecanti Creek and began breaking their own path through the untamed wilderness. With much difficulty they drove up the soft, steep slope of Black Mesa, advancing little more than a foot at a time as both horses and men pushed, lifted, and tugged on the unwilling wagons. While crossing the picturesque table-land, covered with long, thick grass and beautiful forests, they met two men, E. B. Quackenbush and Joseph Brown—future settlers of Paonia —cutting wild hay for the Denver and Rio Grande Railroad Company, which was constructing a railroad through the Black Canyon of the Gunnison from Sapinero to Cimarron.[2]

Chaining their wagon-wheels and tying large, bushy trees behind, the teamsters skidded their wavering wagons down the mesa, camping that night on Crystal Creek. They were surprised to make the disappointing discovery that no fish swam in its clear waters.

"Must be a big fall down the stream somewheres," Hotchkiss remarked, "for this creek should be a trout paradise."[3]

Continuing their journey on the following day, they passed numerous groups of teepee poles standing near the present site of Crawford—mute reminders of a vanished race. The next afternoon the frontiersmen approached the North Fork River a short dis-

[2] The Canyon is so narrow from this point on that it was impossible to build the railroad all the way thru the deep cut.

[3] Because of the water-fall to which Hotchkiss refers, it was necessary to stock the creek before it became the great fishing stream that it is today.

tance below where the town of Hotchkiss now stands.

"I guess I'll be leavin' yuh here for a while," Hotchkiss said. "I'm settlin' across the river a-ways."

"This land around here has good possibilities," observed Samuel, "but I believe that the upper end of the valley is best for fruit-growin'."

"So you think that this valley is goin' to be a fruit country?"

"One of the best," said Samuel, as the two North Fork pioneers parted in different directions.

Samuel led his party along the mesa on the south side of the river, Ezra Wade driving the first wagon into the region. That evening Sam Angevine shot two cub bears, and Paonia's trail-blazers camped on an old Indian cornfield and celebrated their entrance into the "Land of Promise" with a sumptuous feast of bear meat.

With the assistance of Samuel, a skilled surveyor, the explorers spent the remainder of their stay making their claims. Will Clarke and Samuel agreed on a line which later became Grand Avenue as the division between their land, Wade's property extending about half a mile to the west, while Clarke's ranch included most of present Paonia. Ezra Wade located just below his father's claim; Sam Angevine established his preemption rights on the Indian cornfield where Paonia's frontiersmen had spent their first night in the upper valley; George Root pounded his stakes on the farm now belonging to Weldon Hammond, a half-mile north of Paonia, and Joseph Wade settled and first broke soil on the ranch which was later owned by A. L. Roberts, a mile northeast of Paonia.

After returning to Lake City Samuel Wade employed Don Long, Barney Orth, John Roatcap, and his son, John Roatcap, Jr. to haul general merchandise and provisions for the pioneer store of the North Fork, a small dugout on Samuel's ranch.

"It ain't much to look at now," Samuel said one afternoon to his brother Joseph, "but if it develops with the valley, we're gonna have a real store in a little while."

"I hope you're right," replied Joseph, gazing doubtfully at the barren landscape.

"Some day those mesas you're lookin' at will be covered with blooming orchards," Samuel continued. "Before long this whole country will be famous for its fruit."

Joseph turned and looked quizzically at his brother, scratched his head, and wondered.

Those few men who visioned fruit trees among the sage brush and chico of the North Fork set out to make their dreams come true. They immediately made efforts to subdue the hitherto unconquered home of the Utes, who had roamed unmolested for hundreds of years on its unexploited resources, little realizing that their summer hunting grounds would some day be miraculously transformed from a rugged wilderness into a land of blooming orchards and fertile farms.

The virgin country welcomed her new settlers with one of the mildest winters in North Fork history. Loaded wagons crossed Black Mesa during the entire winter of 1881 and 1882 with no difficulty, but in the spring a howling blizzard on the mesa closed travel to all except the most hardy.

Samuel Wade, his sons Frank and Arthur, and Ernest Yoakum made the journey over from Gunnison through the deep snow. They put sled-runners on their wagon and drove their tandem mule team over the frozen snow in the early mornings, stopping them when it became too soft for traveling. In an old trunk Samuel Wade carried a large variety of young fruit trees, and fires were built each night to prevent their freezing. It took the group nearly two weeks to reach their destination near the present site of Paonia, but fortunately the trees were unimpaired. They were set out on Samuel Wade's ranch where some still stand —the last of the fruit-tree pioneers.

Enos Hotchkiss also set out a few fruit trees in the spring of that memorable year, and William Shepherd experimented with some peach-pits. He told W. S. Coburn, most experienced fruit man in the valley, that he had planted them in his spare time out of curiosity with no expectations of ever eating fruit from them.

"Let's hope you've guessed wrong," commented Coburn. "The climate and elevation here are about the same as the great fruit country in the Salt Lake Valley, and if the soil proves anywhere near as fertile, the North Fork should become nationally known for its fruit."

The soil exceeded expectations. By fall Shepherd's seedling peach trees had broken all records in rapidity of growth, evidencing that perhaps Samuel Wade's prophecy to his brother Joseph was not, after all, beyond the realm of possibility.

The next year Samuel Wade, Enos Hotchkiss, and W. S. Coburn shipped several thousand root-grafts into the country and established nurseries which gave birth to the North Fork fruit industry. By 1885 the region began to demonstrate its prolificness, surpassing the wildest hopes of the frontier prophets. In October of that year the first fruit and vegetable show was held under the auspices of the then recently organized Delta County Board of the State Horticultural Society. At this exhibition the newly plowed soil of the North Fork gave one of the most unusual displays ever witnessed.

Spectators gazed in amazement at the rich array of nature's handiwork. Squashes weighing 150 pounds each and pumpkins only slightly smaller[4] lay on the burdened tables beside two and one-half pound onions, thirty-pound beets, and potatoes measuring fourteen inches in length and weighing four pounds apiece. The numerous varieties of apples, peaches, and small fruits were entirely free from pests of any kind. The

[4] Mrs. W. A. Clarke, North Fork pioneer woman, said that she saw one pumpkin which weighed as much as 180 pounds.

Scene at North Fork Fair

—*Courtesy The Paonian*

North Fork Valley seemed destined for fame as an agricultural Utopia.

The fertile, uncorrupted soil and young trees were at their best. Apple trees commonly bore from twenty to thirty boxes of apples in one season, many bearing forty boxes. One acre of pear trees at the average price netted the grower $1,000. Peach trees began producing at the early age of two years[5] and were carrying a full crop in three years—nowhere excelled in flavor or quantity. Charles H. Underwood of Paonia, Civil War captain, raised 945 bushels of potatoes on one acre of land, six selected potatoes weighing sixty pounds, and one of these established a world's record of eleven pounds.[6]

At the Horticultural State Fair of 1890 the North Fork won state-wide recognition for its remarkable productiveness, duplicating the extraordinary exhibit of five years before. No aphis or worms had yet penetrated into this half-civilized land, causing a decided contrast between the North Fork fruit and the pest-bothered specimens from the eastern slope of Colorado. However, the aspirations and dreams of those ambitious pioneers who were staging a victorious battle against the Uncompahgre frontier were not finally realized until Samuel Wade and W. S. Coburn cata-

[5] Guy Hammond, one of the distinguished Hammond brothers of early cowland fame, stated that he saw one seven-inch seedling tree already bearing three peaches.

[6] The potato was molded in wax and placed in the Department of Agriculture at Washington, D. C. The Secretary of Agriculture sent Captain Underwood a personal letter saying that it was the largest potato ever grown so far as any record showed.

pulted this region's reputation across the national headlines by winning six first places at the Chicago World's Fair of 1893 on fruits grown in the virgin soil of the North Fork.

V

SPRING-WAGON EXPRESS

SPRING-WAGON EXPRESS

FROM earliest times Americans have looked forward
to receiving their mail whether it has come by stage-
coach, pony express, spring wagon, or by more modern streamlined zephyrs and airplanes. Today a letter
mailed from New York City to Paonia would probably reach its destination much sooner than one sent
from Delta addressed to the same town in the early
eighties. However, after the spring wagon express was
started, Uncle Sam's mail began traveling the bumpy
road into the North Fork country three times a week.
Through swollen streams, thick adobe mud, and all
kinds of weather the federal carrier bore his sacred
trust so important to residents of the North Fork, and
even in extreme emergencies the unwritten law read
then as now, "The mail must go through!"

During the summer of 1882 the general merchandise in Samuel Wade's dugout was moved into a newly
constructed stockade building near his home. Shortly
thereafter a postoffice was established in one corner
of the store, Samuel Wade becoming postmaster. Samuel was a lover of flowers, many varieties of which he
had brought over and set out on his ranch. The story
is told that he named the postoffice "Peonie" in honor
of his favorite flower, but the government officials

to whom the name was sent designated it as "Paonia," mistaking the e's for a's.

About the same time another postoffice was opened at the residence of Enos Hotchkiss, George H. Duke distributing mail for the lower end of the valley. A short time later it was moved to Joseph Reich's new building, the first store in the town of Hotchkiss.

Two other postoffices also made their appearance. Caleb Maher started one at his ranch house in the Little Muddy or Maher country, walking nearly fifty miles to Sapinero for his contract. Captain Crawford, a knight of the road, was indirectly responsible for the other.

"You know," he observed to Harry Grant, a resident of what is now known as Crawford Mesa, "there oughtta be a postoffice around here to accommodate all them people." He waved his arm toward the farms which dotted the landscape. Grant carried out the transient's suggestion and on May 13, 1883, set up a postoffice in a tent, naming it Crawford after the traveler.

The Denver & Rio Grande Railroad reached Delta from Gunnison in 1882, and the mail was carried from that hamlet into the North Fork by anyone who happened to be journeying up the valley. As a result, the deliveries were very irregular, varying from once to several times a month.

One morning while Samuel Wade and his young son Arthur were en route for Delta, they espied a group of Indians riding single-file up the trail toward them.

"It looks like we'd better get out o' here," Arthur said, pulling back on his bridle reins.

"Don't be afraid, son," Samuel replied. "They'll be more scared than you are."

Suddenly, while still several hundred yards away, the Indian in the lead galloped toward them, holding out a permit as a token of friendship. Samuel took the proffered document, which gave the Utes permission to re-enter their former reservation for the purpose of gathering some horses.

Samuel, who had participated four years in the Sioux War, knew a little of various Indian languages and signs. He told the Indians he had seen their horses on the high mesa above them, now known as Wakefield Mesa. The Ute horsemen started away at a fast pace on their tough little broncos. Several hours later they passed the two white men again, galloping swiftly along behind their herd of mustangs.

Frank Wade was the first paid mail carrier in the valley, the federal government paying him thirty dollars for his three months of service from October to December, 1883. He delivered the mail once a week, riding to Delta on horseback each Saturday and returning the next day. Joseph Reich followed Frank, receiving the earliest contract to carry mail for the North Fork. Reich delivered it three times a week in his spring wagon, introducing the spring-wagon express, which means of transportation was consistently adhered to by his successors.

The responsibility of the express drivers in convey-

ing the mail and express to the postoffices of the North
Fork was accompanied by danger not only from hold-
up men but during certain seasons from the raging
torrents— no respector of lives, property, or bridges.

One afternoon Cal Lewis, driver of the spring-
wagon express, guided a beautiful team of colts into
the North Fork River near the site of the old Paonia
bridge, which a few days before had been washed out
in the spring flood.[1] Crossing along a shallow strip, he
allowed his team to stop and drink. With no warning,
one of them snorted and reared, frightened by a passing drift. Lewis pulled back on the lines with all his
strength as the horse started to run, alarming the
other. Both horses got tangled in their harness as they
plunged in terror down the river toward deep water.
Lewis threw out the mailsacks which were picked up
by Jim Cline, skilled oarsman who lived nearby. Then
Lewis jumped down on the wagon-tongue and cut
the tugs, hoping the colts would be able to swim out.
However, they both drowned as they struggled against
each other and the binding harness—but the mail
reached its readers on time!

In 1889, Thomas C. Wand, from Onarga, Illinois,
erected a building at the south end of Grand Avenue
in Paonia and put in a stock of groceries and dry
goods. The Paonia postoffice was moved to this store,
Wand becoming postmaster. Wade's store quit business, and Samuel devoted his entire time to raising

---

[1] During flood periods, elevated cables and row boats were often used
to transport the early settlers across the swift and treacherous current.

fruit until 1894 when due to failing health he moved to Blaine, Washington, selling his ranch to E. J. Mathews. Nevertheless, the pioneer and founder of Paonia had remained long enough to see the four newly born towns of the North Fork linked with the civilized world by the homely, squeaking spring-wagon express.

VI
THE LIVELY EIGHTIES

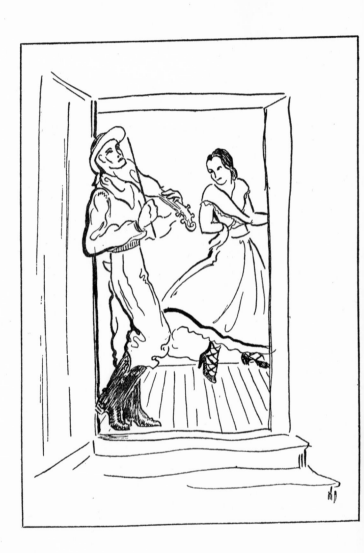

THE LIVELY EIGHTIES

STREAMLINED automobiles, moving pictures, radio, and countless other conveniences and luxuries play a premier part in the high-tensioned twentieth century. Although the ideals and desires of human nature have remained fundamentally the same, the sons and daughters of this scientific age live in an entirely different world from that their antecedents knew fifty years ago. Nevertheless, North Fork pioneers insist that in spite of this miraculous transformation from a primitive to an ultra-modern society there was just as great an opportunity to live an abundant and enjoyable life in the lively eighties as there ever has been since those rough but gay years on the newly opened frontier.

In those dramatic days when square dances reigned supreme, it was much more of an art to swing around the dance floor than it is in our present era of ballroom dancing, where the only prerequisite of a graceful dancer is his ability to keep time to the music. Everybody who could walk, hobble, or ride turned out when Sam Wade's long store was cleared for the Saturday night hops. Those who were not possessed of the desire or the agility to participate would watch the others lithely step to the fiddling and stamp-

ing feet of such local talent as Pap Hightower and
Fiddler Freeman. Whenever available, an organ also
contributed to the merry strains of the fiddle. Wade's
dwelling house was connected with the store, and it
was always a welcome intermission when the gracious
Mrs. Samuel Wade came gliding into the room about
midnight with a large steaming kettle of oyster soup
or other tasty refreshments to rejuvenate the weary
dancers and musicians.

Such forms of entertainment were not always
staged indoors. One unforgettable festival was held
under the waving cottonwoods at Will Clarke's
ranch. An open platform was hastily thrown up for
the dancers, many of whom came before dark while
they could still see the posts which marked the fording lane across the raging North Fork. The party
lasted until daybreak when the wet markers again
became visible to the sleepy eyes of those who had
'danced all night beneath the shining stars to the
awe-inspiring accompaniment of the roaring river.

One of the first dances was held in the fall of
1882 at Enos Hotchkiss's newly constructed house
near Leroux Creek, and every one of the thirty-six
inhabitants of the valley attended. Fiddler Freeman,
big, bearded mountaineer, furnished the rhythm for
most of the early Hotchkiss celebrations. This unusual celebrity scorned farm work as much as he
revered the musical strings of his old violin, and during the summer months he would pack his burros and

Mr. and Mrs. Samuel Wade in 1887

spend his time trapping, hunting, and fishing in the surrounding mountains.

One moonlit Hallowe'en a group of boys discovered Freeman's rickety covered wagon standing peacefully in the sleeping hamlet of Hotchkiss, evidencing the return of the old trapper for the winter. Delighted at their golden opportunity, the boys pulled the wagon several miles up the road with the intention of dumping it over the Rogers Mesa hill. After they had laboriously dragged the old vehicle to the top of the mesa and were preparing to dispose of it on the rocks below, the grinning, bewhiskered face of Fiddler Freeman appeared from within the wagon, re-enforced by a long, rusty flint-lock.

"Thanks for the ride," he said to the astonished culprits, "but it's gittin' 'way past my bedtime, and I think you oughtta start pullin' me back."

The North Fork frontiersmen sometimes had difficulty in locating their church-meetin' clothes to don for the social festivities. One evening Will and Ed Duke, young employees of Enos Hotchkiss, searched through their equipment in an effort to find suitable dress for a dance which was to take place that night. Will finally pulled forth a Prince Albert coat and a pair of white breeches of which he was justly proud in spite of the formidable array of moth holes. His brother, Ed, discovered a suit which he had been packing around for years in a small grip.

With great care and proud miens the two North Fork dudes dressed themselves in their finery. Since no mirror was available, the brothers had to depend on each others' comments as to how they appeared in their "glad rags." Neither had a complete outfit, and in spite of favorable remarks they occasionally took furtive, skeptical glances at each other. When their toilets were completed, they paraded into the mess house by a group of cowboys who had ridden down for the dance. The cowpunchers gazed at the boys for a moment in amazement. Then, suddenly John McIntyre broke the surprised silence with a loud burst of laughter, and soon his companions followed suit, some nearly falling off their chairs in uncontrollable merriment, despite threatening looks from the indignant youths.

For everyday wear the North Fork farmers wore anything they could pull on, and, as a rule, their overalls were decorated with numerous and sundry patches. When George Duke ran out of clothing repairs, he attempted to correct the handicap by cutting off the bottoms of his trouser legs and using the material thus obtained for covering various defects in the seat of the same pair of pants. However, his ingenious plan proved disastrous since he was soon forced to remove so much from the lower extremities that the overalls became too short to tuck into his boots and conceal the deficiency.

The cow-hands were the real dressers of the romantic North Fork. The aristocrats of Louis XV's Versailles Court were not more particular about their attire than these colorful, hard-riding denizens of the

Mountain Fiddler and Friends

cattle range. Fancy high-heeled boots were covered by wool saddle pants made especially for the saddle. Blue, double-breasted, woolen shirts with large pearl buttons on the sides were topped by gaudy-colored handkerchiefs around the neck. Holstered six-shooters flapped against serviceable plain-leather chaps, and wide sombreros were in vogue to shade their tanned faces from the blistering sun.

This vanished race of old-time cowboys had their own particular social gatherings during the long round-ups, the most spectacular being the drinking sprees that occurred during the rides near German Mesa, now called Lamborn Mesa. Some of the German inhabitants of this table-land manufactured luscious homemade wine which they sold to the cowpunchers at one dollar a gallon. The range riders would pass a sombrero from which collection they would purchase as many gallons of sour grape wine as there were dollars in the hat, filling kegs, coffee pots, cups, dishes, and any other liquid-bearing vessel that could be found.

After the day's work the dusty men would line up, and two of the group would volunteer to carry a keg around the circle, pouring its contents into each dry mouth. If a victim didn't swallow fast enough or paused for breath, the beverage would saturate his exterior as well as his interior. As the keg continued to traverse the "bull pen," the keg bearers were relieved whenever they became too tired to move nimbly. Whenever anyone "passed out" he was carried to his welcome blankets, and only the most hardy and practiced lasted to the end. For as long as a week after the revelry the inexperienced drinkers would begin feeling giddy as soon as they started getting warm. However, whenever a rider would roll off his horse in a stupor, some companion would smilingly drag him under the shade of a tree or bush and tie his cow-pony nearby, knowing that when his sleeping partner awakened he would catch up with the slowly driven herd.

Less boisterous affairs were put on by the old fashioned literary societies which staged debates, plays, and readings in the various schoolhouses or in Sam Wade's store. These meetings were held every week or so, and their audiences were from all parts of the valley.

The North Fork conquerors played as hard as they worked, and in spite of their woeful lack of modern facilities and comforts, it is not difficult to understand why many an old-timer's eye sparkles a little brighter than usual when he speaks of the gay night life of a forgotten age.

VII
STANDARD BEARERS

STANDARD BEARERS

THE EARLY settlers were just as anxious to have their offspring learn the "three R's" as are the parents of today. In the fall of 1882 Samuel Wade wrote Jessie Yoakum asking her if she would serve as teacher for the new Paonia schoolhouse in process of construction. Miss Yoakum consented and shortly thereafter boarded the train at Gunnison which traveled the recently built narrow-gauge railroad to Delta. She was met at the depot, a boxcar on a sidetrack, by her brother Ernest, who drove her over the imaginary road to Paonia—which the newcomer justly described as the roughest she had ever seen.

Upon her arrival the ranchers hastened through their farm work so that they could complete the log school building. Paonia's first schoolhouse was about 16 x 24 feet with a wooden floor and glass windows. A box stove rested in the center of the room along the single aisle, wood being used as fuel. Several rows of desks stood before the teacher's stand beside which was placed one of Samuel Wade's office chairs.

School was started during the last week of December, 1882, in order to draw money that year from the Gunnison County school fund to which the North Fork schools were entitled as members of the Gunnison County educational system. Approximately sixteen pupils attended the first session, which lasted three months, Miss Yoakum receiving thirty dollars a month for her services.

A school also was built in Hotchkiss during the fall of 1882, but it was not provided with as many conveniences as its Paonia rival. Holes in the log walls served as windows. Benches were lined up on the dirt floor, each student having a slate on which to draw and write. School commenced the early part of October and lasted six months under the instruction of Etta Gould, pioneer schoolteacher of Hotchkiss.

Church services were conducted in the little log schoolhouses by Father Clark, an old Baptist missionary, who walked his circuit from Crested Butte to Paonia and Hotchkiss and on down the valley about twice a year, boarding at the homes of friends on his long journey. In 1885, needing larger facilities, a new brick building was erected on Grand Avenue in Paonia, and the first school building was abandoned. About this time the Methodist church and the Christian Union were organized, meeting on alternate Sundays in Paonia's brick schoolhouse.

Before the churches were established, when anyone died the frontiersmen made the best of a bad situation and without the assistance of clergymen managed the funeral rites as best they could. In the fall of 1882 Jessie Ennis, a little girl, passed away, and her parents could find no one who would lead the farewell services. Finally, much to everyone's astonishment, L. F.

Upper: Paonia's First Schoolhouse
Lower: Jessie Yoakum in 1883

McAdow, a mysterious cowboy, volunteered to conduct the service.

McAdow had played a lone hand after coming to the North Fork and was an enigma to the inhabitants. Outlaws often drifted into frontier communities, seeking to escape the law in half-civilized and sparsely settled lands. Because no one could persuade him to talk about his past, rumors circulated that this unusual personality was either a bad-man being pursued or a detective in pursuit. Whether they liked him or not, people were intrigued by the impenetrable air of mystery and tragedy that enveloped him. He was well dressed, even when riding after cattle, and seemed highly educated. He "bached"[1] one winter with the gunman, Sam Angevine, and then left, disappearing as strangely and mysteriously as he had come. The funeral of little Jessie Ennis was held in Sam Angevine's cabin, and pioneers who attended the service never forgot the unusual sight as this desperate, unknown character stood beside the body of an innocent child to give her a Christian burial.

The Figure Four outfit, located at the head of Dry Creek near Cedaredge, had adjudicated the water in Leroux Creek and won a permanent right to it in two years, as no one contested their claim. Every summer when the water began getting low, the residents of Rogers Mesa would go to the headwaters of the creek and tear away the dams, diverting the stream to their

[1] Most of the pioneers were bachelors, their Fourth Commandment being, "Six days shalt thou labour and do all thy work, and on the seventh do all thy washing and mending."

dry lands. The Figure Four cow-hands would then ride over to protect their water rights, and numerous free-for-all fights were staged with fists, guns, and clubs. Every winter, H. D. Flack, a Methodist minister from Missouri, came to the North Fork and held revival meetings on the mesa. The worthy farmers then repented for their misdeeds in destroying the dams and fighting the cowboys, but during the subsequent summers when they once more needed water, they would be at it again, harder than ever.

At one of these revivals a big German-Russian, after asking forgiveness for his own sins, began praying for an infamous character on the mesa who had the reputation of being a thief, cattle rustler, and drunkard. "Oh God," pleaded the benefactor, "come down and save dis miserable sinner. But don't send yore son Yesus, for dis is no boy's yob."

These traveling missionaries, rough strangers, and pioneer teachers carried on the early religious and educational activities so necessary in the life of every American community, whether in densely populated sections or on the wild frontier. Without modern equipment, conveniences, or training this advance guard not only carried the burning torch of learning into the rugged wilderness, but served as a medium between man and his God, blazing the way for bigger and more advanced institutions to continue the work so crudely but well started by the early North Fork standard-bearers of civilization and culture.

VIII
COW-LAND ARISTOCRATS

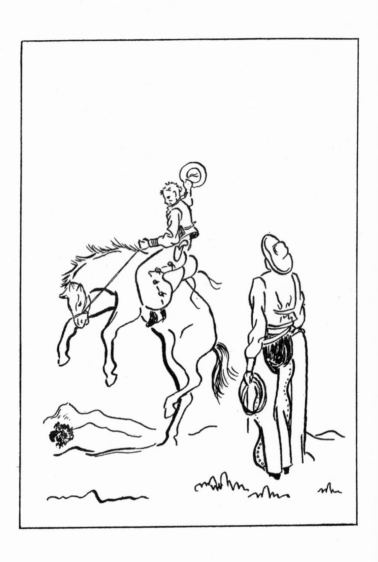

COW-LAND ARISTOCRATS

Sam Hartman, pioneer and early-day cattle king of the North Fork cow-country, started in the cattle business near Denver. During the winter the cattle were allowed to run at large, some of them drifting as far south as the Arkansas River, a distance of nearly 150 miles. Early in May the cowboys would start the big two-months' round-up to gather the cattle and bring them back on the home ranges. Covered wagons were used to haul equipment and "grub", consisting primarily of meat and material for making biscuits. The cook was lord and dictator around the wagon, and every range-rider tried to win his favor and remain in his good graces. Every man furnished his own bedding, which he rolled up and put in the front of the wagon, leaving the back of the vehicle for carrying the food supply.

The chief enemy of the cowpunchers and cattle alike was the predominance of alkali on the southern plains. The KP outfit, owner of 4,000 steers, once lost forty head at on time while watering them on Horse Creek. Due to the strength of alkali in the water holes and streams, the cowboys wore buckskin gloves to protect their hands. Seldom daring to wash in the deadly streams, the riders' faces became nearly as layered with dust as the caked ground on which they rode. The "chuck" wagon always carried a barrel of vinegar on one side, and when the cowhands drank, they put a small quantity of it in their cups to neutralize the alkali. If available, they would also add a teaspoonful of soda and obtain a tasty, fizzing drink, a real treat on the burning plains.

When he was seventeen years old, Sam Hartman traveled from Denver to Saguache in a covered wagon and then rode on horseback along the Old Indian Trail over Cochetopa Pass to the Los Pinos Agency above Gunnison, where his older brother Alonzo was in charge of the distribution of cattle to the Indians on the reservation. From the Los Pinos Agency Sam rode down the Gunnison River to the present site of Sapinero where he turned and followed Soap Creek up to the head of Curecanti. Consequently, he was somewhat acquainted with the possibilities of this territory for raising stock when, three years later—in 1880— he left Denver for Gunnison with the intention of moving into the North Fork and entering the cattle business as soon as the Ute Indians were removed. He drove a large herd of horses over with him, arriving after a two-weeks' trip.

Everything was booming in Gunnison. The mines were all working at full capacity, everyone seemed to have money, and prices were high—flour selling from fifteen to twenty dollars a sack. Sam's brother, Alonzo, was the first postmaster in that city, and his is one of the outstanding names in the annals of Gun-

Sam Hartman in 1888

nison history. Sam made several trips over from Gunnison into the North Fork, and his faith in this country as a great cattle producing region was enhanced when he saw the good condition of the little Indian broncos that the Utes wintered there. When the Uncompahgre reservation, of which the North Fork was a part, was opened to settlers in the fall of 1881, Sam rode over with two hired cow-hands and his brother, Ed, bringing a herd of cattle with them. They met thirty wagons on Black Mesa carrying future settlers into the virgin land.

Sam had been raised in a plains country, and he was fascinated with this fertile mountainous region with its plentiful supply of wood, water, and wild game. He settled in the Little Muddy or Maher section below Castle Rock and built a log shack and a pitch pole fence. The following year he rode back to Gunnison and returned with more cattle, some saddle horses, and a team as well as a plow and 300 pounds of oats—the first seed oats to be planted in the North Fork. In a few years Sam had one of the largest bunches of cattle in western Colorado, running them in the summer months on the Crystal Creek, Curecanti, and Soap Creek ranges, and wintering them on or near his homestead.

By 1883 other stockmen began coming into the North Fork's Utopian grazing land, driving their cattle from Gunnison over Black Mesa via the Old Indian Trail. Aaron Clough and Sam Angevine, buffalo hunter and gunman respectively, put the first cattle on the Minnesota Creek range in 1883. At about the same time David and Solomon Stevens drove a herd into the Holy Terror Creek country while Enos Hotchkiss and the Wade brothers, noted North Fork frontiersmen, were among the first owners of cattle in the big Muddy territory near the headwaters of the North Fork River.

The Shorthorns were the pioneer denizens of the North Fork cow-land, but in the early nineties some Hereford bulls were brought to the Terror Creek range, and before long the Hereford breed outrivalled the Shorthorns because of their earlier development, hardiness, and superior lung power. However, the original Herefords were scrawny appearing animals as compared with their well-built, white-faced successors of today. During the winter months the cattle were driven down from the higher ranges and grazed in the lower country between the newly born towns of Crawford, Paonia, Hotchkiss, and Delta. Approximately 150,000 head roamed Delta county from 1884 to 1890—the heyday of the romantic cattle kings.

About the middle of June the big ride started to round up the cattle, brand the calves, and push the herds up on their summer ranges. As already described in a prior chapter, the cowboys and cattle barons were the recognized blue-bloods of the North Fork in wealth, prestige, and dress. Consequently, it was a highly esteemed honor to be a cow-hand and participate in the long annual round-ups which began at Crystal Creek and then worked Saddle Mountain,

The Start at Hotchkiss for Roundup on Crystal Creek in 1888

Mount Lamborn, upper Minnesota Creek, the Big Muddy, Holy Terror, Leroux, Surface Creek at Cedaredge, and around to the point of Grand Mesa near Grand Junction. Representatives of the various cattle ranches would first assemble at the Diamond Joe cow-camp on Crystal and elect a captain of the round-up who was absolute monarch over the sixty or more horsemen during the entire summer's ride. Sam Hartman often held this position and managed the numerous "punchers" as they rounded up the cattle to brand the calves and push the herds up on their summer ranges. Some old-timers still live who remember the big, picturesque cattleman when he rode the open range, and they all agree that Sam Hartman was the most influential and admired man of the blue-bloods of the cow-country—a king among kings.

However, a man can't always win. When forty-five years old, Sam jumped for the step of a moving road wagon and fell, his knee slipping through the spokes of a wheel. He reached for the lines as he fell back on his side but stopped the team too late. With remarkable stamina he managed to drag himself into the wagon and drive back to the ranch house where he fell over on the seat in a dead faint. A doctor was summoned from the nearest town. No other suitable instrument being available, he sawed off the mangled leg with one of the ranch's dehorning saws. Sam took the loss of his leg with poker-faced equanimity, and if he felt unkindly towards Lady Luck, he kept it to himself.

The cards continued to fall against him. His investments crashed. He borrowed money to buy cattle when the market was high, and then beef prices collapsed. Sam lost nearly everything he owned, but in the same nonchalant manner with which he bore the loss of his leg he continued to play each hand dealt him as best he could, never glorifying his brilliant past nor complaining about the unpromising future. Conditions were never again the same for him as during those golden days when he led his hard-riding cow-punchers across the unfenced frontier, but until the end, Sam retained one holdover from the old West—that unconquerable spirit of the genuine pioneer, tamer of the wilderness.[1]

In the fall another round-up was staged to gather beef and push the rest down into the valley for the winter because of the heavy snowfalls in the mountains. The beef were then taken to Delta, Glenwood Springs, or driven over Black Mesa along the Old Hartman Trail to Sapinero and shipped by rail to market. Sam Hartman herded part of his beef cattle to Glenwood Springs to supply that town with meat, the journey taking from five to six days. Nevertheless, those old-time "cow-pokes" usually made the trip without the loss of a single head.

The last big summer round-up occurred in 1893. By this time the winter ranges were largely fenced in or overgrazed, and thousands of cattle died during the winter from starvation. As many cattle kings failed

[1] Sam came by this spirit naturally since he was a direct descendant of another great pioneer, Daniel Boone.

to adapt themselves to a changing West and were being forced out of business leaving unoccupied range, the cattlemen's sovereignty over the North Fork grazing domain started being contested, and a new and bitter struggle began which has continued up to the present day and is tied up with the subsequent history of the cattle industry.

The sanguinary feuds between sheep and cattle men have colored the North Fork stock region with blood and adventure since the arrival of the first flock of unwelcome foreign sheep on to the unregulated range. Due to unscientific grazing practices and lack of governmental restrictions in the early days, cattle producers had to battle powerful interests in order to keep their land free from destroying herds of sheep which continually clamored for entrance into the coveted superior ranges of the cow-country. Sheep are notorious for their ability to close-crop and tramp down the most heroic growth of wild grass and foliage if allowed to remain on one bed-ground for any length of time. Old-time herders were a plague to any feeding grounds because most of them would graze their flocks in the same spots for weeks at a time, transforming luscious green pastures to desolate desert. With blazing rifles and six-guns the western Colorado Night Riders held back for a while the menacing tide of migratory sheep, but this mysterious group of cattlemen and cowboys were playing against a stacked deck—falling beef prices, depletion of their winter ranges by homesteaders, and opposition of the federal government, which appropriated control of the disputed lands from sympathetic local officials.

From 1884 to 1890 the cattle industry boomed, but in the nineties conditions became less favorable to cattle producers. Sheepmen had long looked with envious eye on the rich feed which grew so abundantly in this section. In the summer of 1893 some Utah men brought 6,000 head of sheep into the North Fork. Their unexpected appearance took the cattlemen by surprise, but they were not long in informing the visitors that this was not a healthy sheep climate. As the bleeting flocks were being driven out, heavily armed cowboys gathered at various conspicuous places to encourage continuation of the sheep herders' hasty progress off the cattle range.

As other Utah sheep outfits attempted to establish themselves in western Colorado, a secret organization sprang up to resist by force this threatened invasion. This occult army of anti-sheep men called themselves the Cattle Growers' Protective Association, but possibly because of their nocturnal campaigns, they became more commonly known as the Night Riders. This secret society had members in nearly every cow-camp on the Western Slope, including the territory of Meeker, Glenwood Springs, Grand Junction, Whitewater, the North Fork, Montrose, and Gunnison. Each locality had its own local association which acted as a vigilante committee. Whenever some newly arrived foreign sheep herd appeared, the information was sent to some far away committee which would

Enos Hotchkiss's Sheep on Big Muddy

send out a group from their own number to the tres-
passed region. These men would take a pack outfit,
extra saddle horses, and guns, traveling singly or in
pairs so as not to attract attention.

Upon gathering at some seclusive rendezvous, they
would make their plans as to the most effective means
of obtaining their objective. The local Night Riders
would not usually participate in the subsequent ex-
pulsion since they were too well known in the vicinity.
Since the calling of outside help was often done as a
last resort, extreme measures were usually in order.
Shooting hot lead into the hated flocks as well as an
occasional resisting Mexican herder was the most common method of starting the undesirable guests on the
homeward trail. One of the biggest massacres occurred
in the White River country near Meeker when the
Night Riders, so it was said, greeted an incoming outfit by killing 2,000 of their sheep as the giant herd
was being stampeded off the range.

In spite of the cattlemen's antipathy towards sheep,
they never objected to those owned by Enos Hotchkiss, North Fork pioneer, on the Big Muddy. However, this sacred flock held a respect never conferred
on alien sheep by the hardy cowpunchers of the North
Fork. Many were the casualties that happened to venturesome sheepmen who attempted to escort their innocent wards into the North Fork cattle country. One
incoming herd was met near the state bridge, which
crosses the Gunnison River between Hotchkiss and
Delta, and the yelling cowboys tried to run the terri-

fied sheep over a nearby high bluff. Shortly afterwards another group of unidentified riders turned
back several thousand near Gunnison by mowing
down the flocks with high-powered rifles and six-
shooters. The Night Riders were not responsible for
all of these encounters with adventurous sheepmen,
but since those belonging to the Cattle Growers' Protective Association took an oath to never divulge any
of its activities under penalty of death, it is difficult
to determine where their escapades left off and the
missions of independent local cowhands began. Two
members of the cabalistic organization broke their
oath of secrecy on the witness stand in a trial at
Montrose for sheep killing, and on the following night
they were forcibly taken out of jail and disappeared
forever.

The sheepmen retaliated for these none too gentle
repulses in many ways. During one of the fracases a
cowboy dropped a pair of fringed buckskin gloves
with his name embroidered on the back. A few days
later his haystacks were burned to the ground. Dead
cattle were found on numerous "stomp" grounds—
poisoned or shot. Once an invisible sharpshooter
spilled a hailstorm of bullets into a large corral
jammed with several hundred bawling steers. All
these catastrophes were a part of the cattle and sheep
war resulting from the ungoverned range. In spite
of these reprisals and the gradual fencing in of their
winter ranges by homesteaders the cattle interests continued to be victorious.

During the first decade of the twentieth century the forest service was established, abolishing the evils of unregulated range in the higher country, but the fighting continued in a legal form. With the rapid decline of beef prices and a rise in the sheep market in 1915 many North Fork residents, including some of the former Night Riders, asked the forest service to allow sheep on the ranges. In that same year a meeting was called at Hotchkiss to discuss the controversy of allotting permits to graze sheep on the forest reserve left vacant by cattlemen who had been unable to meet the changing conditions of depleted range and low prices. Grazing supervisors presided at this momentous assembly and listened to the arguments of the opposing groups. In spite of the pressure brought to bear by the powerful American Wool Growers' Association, the government officials were at first in favor of continuing their former policy, but when a number of local men insisted that they as citizens and pioneers of the region had equal rights with the cattlemen to the unoccupied territory, the Forester decided that it was time to initiate a new plan of action.

As a result of this gathering, sheep were permitted on the forest reserve wherever the grazing supervisor saw fit at a ratio of five sheep to one cow, local men to be given preference in the subsequent issuance of sheep permits. The Big Muddy section and country at the headwaters of the North Fork River were shortly thereafter opened to sheepmen. The inexperienced

North Fork residents who wished to venture in the
lucrative sheep business were primarily responsible
for the introduction of the unfamiliar flocks on the
old cattle grounds, but after two or three years these
novice sheepmen quietly passed out of the picture
as their stock became less profitable, giving outsiders
their long-awaited opportunity to obtain a foothold
on the North Fork's grassy fields. They proceeded to
buy out many sheep and cattle ranches, exchanging
sheep for cattle at the required ratio. Due to careless
grazing practices, the Big Muddy range was permanently injured by its new denizens, but the other
North Fork feeding grounds, including the Holy Terror, Minnesota, and Crystal Creek ranges, have so far
remained largely closed to the ever watchful sheep
interests.

The public domain, consisting of the lower grazing
lands, continued to go unrestricted long after the
forest service had been started. By 1917 the Gunnison River was the recognized dividing line between
the sheep and cattle country near Sapinero, the north
side belonging by the unwritten law to the cattle
barons while the south side was occupied by the sheep
lords. After the bleating flocks had tramped down
their feed, they threatened to cross over the stream
into the more tempting pastures of the well-fed Herefords. In 1918 the Mexican herders finally summoned
sufficient courage to drive their hungry hordes across
the Gunnison into enemy territory. For many nights
following, the herders dared not sleep in their tents

but kept all night vigils in surrounding hideouts. The national government finally became cognizant of the dangerous strife on the public domain, and on June 18, 1934, the Taylor Grazing Act was enacted which put this contested territory under federal supervision, thereby ending the notorious feudal warfare on the western hills and prairies. Today, due to nationally protected ranges and increased scientific grazing restrictions, more harmony exists between the cattle and sheep rivals than when the mystic riders of the night patrolled the open range under the western stars. Not only is there less resentfulness as to sharing the same ranges but certain progressive stockmen are beginning to demonstrate the advantages of engaging in the production of both beef and mutton.

In the early days cattle were run at practically no expense with the result that every cow which was sold brought a profit regardless of the purchase price. Consequently, the big annual losses and poor quality of the stock were more than offset by the lack of expenditure and the large number of cattle owned by the cattle kings. However, with the forfeiture of their old winter ranges it became necessary for those cattlemen who remained in business to keep their stock fenced in during the winter and feed them hay. This created a real expense which necessitated a sharp reduction in the size of their herds. It soon became evident that if the cow-business was ever again going to be profitable that the new costs of production and lack of quantity must be compensated by a minimum loss and a high grade of cow.

To accomplish these objectives only registered bulls were allowed on the range, and gradually the mixed breeds and culls were weeded out and shipped to market so that after years of scientific effort the North Fork cattle of today have been built up to nearly a pure-bred quality. During the winter and early spring they are kept on the ranches where they are fed and watched carefully to reduce loss as much as possible, for with the cost of feeding, ranch expenses, and the payment of high property taxes a few head may weight the scales to either a profit or a deficit in the annual account books.

In the spring the beautiful, well-marked herds are driven from the ranches on to the public domain. As the larkspur and other poisonous weeds of the forest reserve become less prevalent during the summer months, the cattle are gradually pushed up on their picturesque summer ranges, and the old West lives again as twentieth century cowboys gallop their trained, well-bred horses across the still untamed cowland on shorter but none-the-less romantic round-ups to brand the calves and direct the herds farther and farther up on the reserve as the lower regions are grazed down.

Every fall the cattle are gathered at the cow-camps where the eligible fat steers and cows are sorted out for shipment and the remainder driven down to the ranches. The beef are then herded to the local stock-

Upper: Modern Cattle on Crystal Creek Range
 —Courtesy Daily Record Stockman
Lower: Hunting Scene on Minnesota Creek Range

yards, loaded on cattle cars, and shipped to the central markets where they are sold by commission houses. The cow-country of yesterday has changed, but the color of the historic West has not faded amid the lofty, unconquered mountains of the North Fork.

IX
COW-TOWN

COW-TOWN

CRAWFORD is unique and ranks among the most individualistic villages of Colorado. It is one of those few remaining cow-towns which today are seldom seen outside of Hollywood studios. Genuine cowpunchers with wide sombreros and high-heeled boots lounge around its board sidewalks. Excited herds of cattle en route to their winter ranches, spring ranges, and the fall markets stampede through its steep, cowtracked main street. Drowsy cow-ponies stand tied to old western hitching rails, and horsemen are as commonly seen on its streets as automobiles.

This unusual town has the added distinction of lying entirely on the side of a high hill. The story is told that its pioneer inhabitants built on the nearly precipitous slope in order to save the surrounding level flats for farming purposes as well as to obtain water more easily from the nearby Smith Fork of the Gunnison. The main street is so steep that motorists often find it necessary to go through the business district in second gear, and woe betide the unfortunate driver who tries to park for shopping purposes if the brakes of his automobile are not in good working order. This hill-town is the trading center for the largest cattle section of the North Fork, including the Maher, Crystal Creek, and Smith Fork country. Although predominately a cattle-land, there are also a few sheep outfits in the region.

The present site of Crawford was a barren hillside until 1892. The early settlers in its neighborhood depended originally upon the country's game for a living. The wild life not only provided them with food until they could get established, but the San Juan mining camps and Black Canyon railroad crew, who constructed the Denver and Rio Grande Railroad through a portion of the deep cut in 1882, furnished a good market for meat.

Soon after the North Fork was opened for settlement, Clower Freeman built a small store near Crystal Creek along the main road. This frontier supply station became a stopping-off place for incoming settlers and travelers besides furnishing the pioneer inhabitants along Crystal Creek, who then lived there the year around, with necessary provisions. In 1883 Theodore Kremling purchased the frontier store. Among his best customers were the Diamond Joe and other early-day range riders.

In the early eighties two postoffices sprang up in this newly settled portion of the North Fork. Cabel Maher established one at his ranch house during 1882 in the Little Muddy or Maher country, walking nearly fifty miles to Sapinero for his contract. The postoffice was moved around to the residence of every newly appointed postmaster for thirty-six years. In 1918 Paul

Kremling, brother of Theodore Kremling, constructed the first Maher postoffice building. It is still in use.

Captain Crawford, a knight of the road, while traversing the North Fork region a year or so after it was opened for settlement made his temporary camp on what is now known as Crawford Mesa.

"You know," he remarked to Harry Grant, a resident of the mesa, "there oughtta be a postoffice around here to accommodate all them people." He waved his arm toward the farms which dotted the landscape. Grant carried out the transient's suggestion and on May 13, 1883, set up a postoffice in a tent, naming it Crawford. Two years later Joseph Preston, Crawford's second postmaster, moved it to a little log cabin beside the Smith Fork.

In the mid-eighties the first Crawford school-house was built near the ranch now owned by Everett Porter. Harry Grant was Crawford's first school teacher as well as its pioneer postmaster. Two other country schools appeared soon afterward within a few miles of the Crawford schoolhouse, one on Crawford Mesa and the other near the Clear Fork. Each of these school districts had its literary society around which revolved the early social life. These organizations staged debates, plays, and other performances in the school buildings every week or so.

The Crystal Creek trading post was the only one in the region until 1892 when the twice-married Mrs. Elizabeth Ong opened the first store in the present city limits of Crawford. Until then the growing town

of Hotchkiss was the chief commercial center for the
Smith Fork and Crystal Creek cow-country. This was
true not only because Hotchkiss was the largest town
in the valley but also because the only road reached
it before turning off to the smaller village of Paonia,
ten miles up the river.

The largest business house in the entire North Fork
during its early settlement was the Duke brothers' establishment in Hotchkiss. This store carried nearly
$100,000 worth of general merchandise, including dry
goods and notions, groceries, clothing, boots and shoes,
and machinery. During the spring floods when the
raging North Fork River prevented the Crawford
ranchers from reaching Hotchkiss, they journeyed
over Black Mesa to Sapinero, a hamlet named in honor
of Chipeta's brother, to do their trading.

When Mrs. Ong started her store in Crawford, she
was about forty-five years old, plump, outspoken, and
self-reliant. Whenever she needed a fresh supply of
goods, she would hitch up her team and drive thirty-
five miles to acquire her commodities at Delta. The
thought of hiring a man to make the tedious trip for
her apparently never entered her economical head.
Desiring lumber, she would drive up to the saw mills
on Black Mesa and load it herself, further evidencing
her businesslike and thrifty temperament even when
it involved doing a man's work. The masculine members of the Crawford neighborhood soon learned to
respect her caustic tongue and dared not cross her in
any business dealings for fear of a verbal lashing. Con-

CRAWFORD, COLORADO
Upper View, 1892; Lower, 1929

sequently, she usually got her own way and became the dominating center of the community.

Her youthful son, Floyd Zimmerman, assisted in the store, and his exceptional courtesy to the customers offset the brusqueness of his mother. In 1896 Paul Kremling went into partnership with Mrs. Ong. A rival store made its appearance on the opposite side of the Smith Fork a year later, but before long it was moved across the creek to double the size of Crawford's shopping quarter.

During 1901 a road was constructed a few miles below Crawford over the adobes to Paonia, decreasing the distance between the two towns by five miles, which in those horse and buggy days saved two hours on a round trip. This short-cut was an additional stimulus to Paonia's rapid growth by increasing its trade with the Crawford country; however, it was not until 1904 that Paonia's population increased beyond that of Hotchkiss.

Crawford grew steadily after 1897. Five years later two blacksmith shops, two stores, a church, and a small hotel could be counted within its city limits. As the North Fork developed, lumber came to be more and more in demand for building purposes. The mills in the Black Mesa, Dyer Fork, and Crystal Creek regions provided Crawford and Hotchkiss with lumber. Frank Lambertson, George Goodwin, the Flukes, the Bells, De Long, and Edward Schoneman established the pioneer mills in this cow-land. Government officials were sent in to determine the amount of timber in this country. In one section of 640 acres about two miles above Frank Lambertson's mill on Dyer Fork, they estimated 30,000,000 feet of lumber. The mills and box factories on Terror and Hubbard creeks kept Paonia provisioned in the early years of its settlement.

By 1907 Crawford had reached its full growth of approximately 160 inhabitants and had become the recognized trading center of one of the larger cattle districts of Colorado. While Crawford has today most of the modern conveniences and well-equipped, up-to-date homes, it is intrinsically still as much of a cow-town as it was fifty years ago—true home of the modern vassals of the saddle.

X
FRUIT UTOPIA

FRUIT UTOPIA

AFTER the North Fork fruit industry leaped into the national limelight at the Chicago World's Fair of 1893, fruit culture began rivaling cattle production as the leading occupation of the region. Professor H. E. Van Deman, United States pomologist, noted this rapid development in his 1893 report to the Department of Agriculture:

> The fruit interest here is beginning to override all others, and orchards are being planted in every direction. The table-lands, or mesas, are entirely free from alkali properties and seem to be best for fruit. They are extremely well adapted to all kinds of deciduous fruits. The peach, apricot, and all the deciduous fruits were bearing profusely. No insect enemies were seen or heard of in this vicinity.

Encouraged by success at the World's Fair, North Fork fruit was entered in competition at the Trans-Mississippi Exposition of 1898 in Omaha, Nebraska, and again the large, highly colored, perfect specimens from this region won gold medal awards against the largest and most varied array of horticultural displays since the World's Fair five years before.

Experienced agriculturists began to visit this highly proclaimed, little known land of the colored fruits, curious to view the country about which so many improbable stories were told. However, the fondest expectations of the astonished newcomers were surpassed at the sights they witnessed in the quiet, unpretentious little valley. H. M. Stringfellow, horticulturist expert from Galveston, Texas, reflected the consensus of opinion when, in 1898, he made an official statement to the *North Fork Times* of Hotchkiss, only newspaper in the North Fork at the time:

> I can only express myself with wonder at the North Fork country. I have never seen anything like it in my life, and believe that it will become the wonderland of the fruit industry. As much as I have traveled, and as familiar as I am with horticultural sections of our country and results attained by them in quantity and quality, no section that I am acquainted with can make such a showing.

Lady Fortune continued to smile on the newly settled area. In 1899 many fruit districts throughout Colorado and the nation were severely impaired by frosts and drouths, but the North Fork had its most prolific growth in the face of the surrounding disasters. As a result, representatives from the leading commercial houses of Chicago, St. Louis, Omaha, and numerous other western mercantile centers came to the North Fork to compete for its fruit products, especially the late varieties of peaches and apples. The Jonathan and Winesap apples had replaced in popularity the Ben Davis,[1] which up until this time had been the grower's bank account. The Elberta peach

[1] In a letter to Mr. Coburn, W. N. White & Co., New York exporters of fruit, wrote: "Your Jonathans and Winesaps are without exception the finest in the United States."

Fruit Wagons Arriving in Delta in 1895

predominated its field, with the Crawford and Mountain Rose close seconds, while the Bartlett pear outclassed all rivals in its species.

The frontier fruit raisers originally sold most of their produce to peddlers who peddled their tasty wares in surrounding mining towns, particularly the booming San Juan gold and silver camps of Ouray, Telluride, Rico, Red Mountain, Silverton, Lake City, Ophir, and Saw Pit. The local men, engaged in other types of work, also provided a market. After the fertile North Fork had demonstrated its superiority as a fruit country, orchards began increasing rapidly, and before long the supply of fruit exceeded the local and peddling demands. Since the nearest railroad was thirty-five miles away at Delta, a real problem arose as to the best means of disposing of the surplus.

When commissioners from various western commercial houses began soliciting North Fork fruit, the ranchers started hauling their excess goods to Delta, where they sold them to competing buyers. Since no packing houses were then available, the fruit was boxed for shipment by crews in the orchards where picked. At first there had been hesitation about packing and transporting peaches by wagon to Delta since the common supposition prevailed that so soft a fruit could not endure the jolting trip and still be salable. Finally one venturesome farmer, who particularly disliked seeing his fine-looking peaches wasted, made the effort, and much to his and everyone's surprise, his peaches reached Delta in good condition.

As many as sixty-five fruit-laden wagons in a row came to be a common sight along the bumpy road to Delta—men, horses, and wagons transformed to the same white color by the alkali dust which hung in the air so thickly that the road could be traced all the way across the barren adobes. The anxious buyers often met the incoming vendors ten or twelve miles from Delta in the hope of consummating a bargain before the competition became too strenuous as they approached town. In 1895 Arthur Wade drove into the buzzing town and auctioned off thirty-three wagon loads of Elberta peaches, the first straight carload of this type to be shipped from Delta.

During these gala years the supply of fruit was small in this western country and the resultant demand so great that the North Fork fruitmen could practically set their own prices. W. T. Hawkey of Paonia, for example, with less than twenty acres of bearing orchard and many of his trees not yet old enough to bear a full crop netted $2,775 in 1896 with 1,500 pounds of pears yet to be sold. Single peach trees in Samuel Wade's and W. S. Coburn's orchards commonly produced fruit that sold from fifteen to twenty dollars per tree. The expense of production was much less than today due to the absence of insect enemies which had not as yet become a problem. This was the primary reason for the large net returns.

At the turn of the century, 1900 to 1901, thousands of additional acres were planted in fruit upon the speculation that a branch railroad would be constructed from Delta to the Utopian fruit district of the North Fork. The approaching boom was rapidly gathering momentum.

The first North Fork settlers staked out their claims along the river and creek bottoms and dug little irrigating ditches from the nearby streams to their ranches. After the choice lowlands were settled, longing eyes began looking up at the fertile but waterless mesas. When the fruit industry started prospering, the feeling became more and more prevalent that the higher lands must be conquered.

Edd Hanson began the canal-digging epoch by financing the Farmers Ditch in the late eighties to bring water over a twelve-mile course along the north side of the river to what is now known as Hanson Mesa, which extends westward almost to the town of Hotchkiss. However, it was not until the North Fork won national recognition at the Chicago World's Fair of 1893 that canal construction really commenced in earnest. Early in September, 1894, one of the great enterprises in western Colorado ditch-building was started by George Stewart and his father, D. J. Stewart, newcomers from Webb City, Missouri.

Seeing there was insufficient water to suitably irrigate the property they contemplated buying, the two promoters made surveys in order to determine the feasibility of a large irrigation project. Having ascertained that such a plan was practicable, they set out to bring life-producing water to 2,200 acres of unimproved land lying south of the North Fork River.

The headgate of this canal was placed four miles above Paonia where it received its water supply from the winding North Fork. When completed, in 1896, the Stewart ditch, appropriately named in honor of its founders, extended a length of ten miles with a 4½-foot fall to the mile. It passed over 11,000 feet of fluming, had a capacity of 1,000 cubic feet per second, and measured ten feet across the bed.

Small green patches were developed here and there along the highlands above and beyond the Farmers Ditch by directing the water from a few mountain streams to the dry, unproductive soil. Rogers Mesa, wide plateau a mile west of Hotchkiss, for example, derived a small supply from Leroux Creek. As its population increased, the lack of sufficient water became more and more noticeable. The residents dug reservoirs in the hills above to help replenish the annual shortage, but they continued to run short. The exceptionally dry year of 1896 made it imperative that more drastic measures be taken. Notices were posted around Hotchkiss requesting that all those interested in obtaining more water for Rogers Mesa meet at the school house. This sparsely attended meeting was the modest beginning of an even larger undertaking than the Stewart Ditch, which was nearing completion.

No development in the region took more courage and stamina than the building of the Fire Mountain Canal.[2] It was one big ditch that was constructed en-

---

[a] So named because it is cut across a mountain in whose troubled interior vast quantities of hidden coal have been burning for thousands of years.

North Fork Orchard Scene

tirely by the local people, who furnished both the
capital and labor. Contributions were made by the
bankers and merchants, the returns from their investment being stock in the ditch. The work was done
by ranchmen who left their farms during the winter
months, when their orchards and fields did not need
attention, to dig through the frozen ground. Wages
were low, most of which were payable in stock. At the
company's yearly gathering in 1897 the secretary's
report stated that of the 10,463 shares of capital stock
that had been issued, 9,620 were for labor. No eight-
hour-day laws were then in vogue, and the men will-
ingly worked from daybreak to sunset, averaging
about twelve hours a day, even though, so it has been
said, the impoverished treasury was not always able to
keep the workers provided with enough to eat. The
contributions and assessments were just sufficient to
keep the plows sharpened, settle blacksmith bills, and
pay a minimum salary. Not a stick of dynamite was
used on the entire length of the canal through forma-
tions of cement, shale, boulders, and hillsides. The
rocks had to be pried out by hand and rolled away
with teams. However, the North Fork ranchers were
not afraid of toil and hardships, and at one time the
laborers numbered sixty men with teams, the line
reaching a mile long. Ed Duke superintended the job
for the first four miles, riding back and forth among
the workers on horseback.

Ground was first broken in September, 1896, and
it took five strenuous years to complete the Fire

Mountain Canal. When finished, it wound thirty-two miles along the north side of the North Fork River, from which stream the canal's water supply was obtained about ten miles above Paonia. This ditch carried the valuable life-giving liquid to Rogers, Sunnyside, and Pitkin mesas, reclaiming nearly 10,000 acres of the thirsty highlands a mile or more above the level of the Farmers Ditch. Blooming orchards and green fields stand today as living monuments to the Spartanic sacrifices of the Fire Mountain Canal builders.

The Duke brothers of Hotchkiss were the chief promoters of the Overland Ditch, which was begun about the same time as the Fire Mountain Canal. Most of the dark, sandy loam on Redlands Mesa, six miles northwest of Hotchkiss, was filed on under the Desert Land Act by those who had faith in the completion of the project, including the Redlands Orchard Company which planned to set out a large commercial orchard of apples, peaches, and pears. When the twenty-one-mile ditch was finished, approximately 9,000 acres of mesa land were ready for cultivation.

At the beginning of the present century a reservoir was dug in Onion Valley, about twenty-five miles south of Paonia, near Maher, Colorado. This reservoir was constructed so as to have a storage capacity of 8,000 acre feet behind a sixty-foot dam. A ditch twenty miles long was built from it to rejuvenate about 10,000 acres of barren land which lay just south of the Smith Fork of the Gunnison and extended ten miles down the creek from the nearby town of Crawford. This tableland was labeled Fruitland Mesa, evidencing the early belief that the North Fork fruit boom would transform this plateau into a fruit section. However, the soil and altitude did not prove suitable for ideal orchard growth, and many local wits now refer to the mesa, which produces hay and grain, by the more appropriate title of "Fruitless" Mesa.[3]

Railroad commission houses were ready to handle the North Fork fruit when the train first pulled into Hotchkiss and Paonia during the fall of 1902, ending forever the long lines of wagon shipments to Delta. The coming of iron rails was the real beginning of Paonia's boom which lasted until about 1911 when Robert W. Curtis sold ten acres of peach land for $3,500 an acre. During this period it was not unusual to buy ranches at $1,000 an acre and in two weeks sell them for $1,200 an acre. One orchard consisting of twenty-two acres of apples and five acres of peaches returned $27,000 in the three years of 1904, 1905, and 1906.

This golden prosperity was not only due to the new railroad, mild climate, the soaring reputation of the North Fork fruit country, and the splendid market, but also to insistent advertising. Real estate men hired the publisher of the *Paonia Newspaper* alone to print

---

[3] Although the North Fork mesas are now green with their newly found life, the local water question is still a problem. By the first of July eighty-five per cent of the water is gone while fifty per cent of the need remains thereafter. After July only ten per cent of the total annual flow of streams can be used. If reservoirs were built to save this now wasted spring and early summer surplus, the production of the North Fork Valley would be greatly increased.

480,000 six-page folders to publicize the valley. These were printed in red and blue ink with an optimistic write-up of the region. Each pamphlet was small enough to fit a large envelope, and they were circulated freely not only by the real estate men but by every citizen of the valley, who enclosed them with their correspondence. This widespread advertising played a major part in the rapid rise of land values.

From 1904 to 1909 nearly everyone was planting fruit, and the mesas as well as the bottom-lands soon became one continuous garden of blooming orchards. Paonia grew swiftly, developing in population from about 250 at the beginning of the boom period to over four times that size by 1909, surpassing its rival town, Hotchkiss, which had grown from about 300 to 650 inhabitants. During 1904 to 1907 three weekly newspapers ran in Paonia at the same time, their enthusiastic publishers believing, like many others, that the rapidly growing town would soon develop into a metropolis. The *Paonia Newspaper* was established by C. T. Rawalt on August 12, 1904 as a six-column, four-page news sheet, Democratic and liberal in politics. The *Paonia Booster*, started in June, 1904, by Charles Adams and Clinton L. Oliver, was solidly Republican, while C. A. Frederick's *Paonia Gazette*, initiated in 1900 as the first paper in Paonia, prided itself on taking no sides in any political feuds or strife whatsoever. In 1912 Arthur L. Craig, the present editor, purchased the *Paonia Booster* and changed its name to *The Paonian*. A few months later the *Paonia News-*

PAONIA, COLORADO
Upper View, 1900; Lower, 1930

paper, only remaining news sheet, was suspended, and *The Paonian* alone continued.

The first newspaper in the North Fork, the *North Fork Times,*[4] made its appearance May 21, 1897, in Hotchkiss, largest town of the valley at that time. The opening editorial in the first edition is of particular interest:

In launching the craft to be known as the North Fork Times upon the sea of the journalistic world, it is perhaps proper for the publishers to introduce to their readers the relative position we propose to occupy in the field as a newsgatherer and our prospective relations to the locality where it is situated.

The Times will introduce thru its columns reliable and effective information of the resources and the advantages of the North Fork to the prospective settlers from time to time; we also realize that our interests are identical with Delta county and the Western Slope in general.

We believe in our own fireside first but in being loyal and reasonable towards other localities.

It is to be strictly understood that no political party, corporation, firm, individual, or other combination has any strings on us.

This paper is edited and published as a commercial proposition in its strictest sense. Slander, vituperation, and vindictiveness of political or social character will find no place in our columns. It is proposed by the publishers to furnish, at all times, reliable and wholesome reading matter, such as will appeal to the intelligent portion of the community.

The first publication will be a fair sample of future copies. In conclusion we only ask fair and liberal treatment at the hands of our businessmen and agricultural classes and in return we will give you a first-class paper. In addition it is our purpose to encourage enterprises and improvements that will tend to make the town of Hotchkiss a place of importance.

[4] Its publisher was Rudolph Lossius.

Fickle Fortune does not usually long remain faithful to those on whom she lavishes her much-courted
good graces. As if expecting the seclusive mountain
valley of the North Fork to become the long-sought-
after but never discovered Shangri-la of humanity,
she protected it for a while from the ravages of life
and time. Then, apparently deciding suddenly that
the ideal Utopia which she visualized could never be
completely attained, she turned away to let rough
nature take its normal course.

The inherent laws of economics and climatic conditions did not continue to be so kind to the North
Fork. The great fruit country of the Northwest was
occupied during the fore part of the twentieth century, and before long surpluses were thrown on the
western fruit market, lessening the demand for North
Fork products. Until 1905 this section never had
known anything in the way of a general failure, and
everyone raised a full crop. As more and more orchards
were planted, the North Fork produced more than the
railroad could carry, and much fruit was lost through
delay in shipping. A freeze occurred in 1912 which
devastated the entire region and killed most of the
peach trees. This calamity hastened the fall in real
estate values. Fruit-destroying pests had gradually become a serious problem, greatly increasing the costs of
production. As prices continued to drop in the face
of rising expenses, many fruitmen sold out and left
the country. Thousands of fruit trees were pulled out,
and the land was used for general farming. Retired

businessmen and farmers who had come to the North Fork and invested their savings in orchards, hoping to spend the rest of their lives in security and comfort, lost nearly everything they owned.

By 1913 the North Fork had passed through the visionary mists of paradise into a severe depression. Although the valley subsequently recovered from the panic, the production of fruit today is only from a quarter to a third as much as it was from 1906 to 1909, height of the boom epoch. The Utopian days have passed forever, but the North Fork still has the climate, water, and soil to rank it even yet among the champion fruit districts of the nation.

XI
BLACK TREASURE

BLACK TREASURE

THERE are about 371 billion tons of coal in the state of Colorado.[1] Of this amount approximately 333 billion tons, largely unmined, lie amid the scenic beauties of the Western Slope. The North Fork coal lands probably have the wealthiest resources of any section. Nevertheless, the early settlers in this region were unaware of the vast quantities of hidden black treasure around them. Wood was used entirely for fuel, and even the newly established blacksmith shops burned overgrown willows to make their charcoal. However, it was not destined that the silent mountains should long keep their secret.

In the early eighties Niles Sylvester filed on land which included the present Oliver mine and employed a man to live there and hold it for him. The river had washed into a vein of coal near this tract, exposing the dusky fuel. Sylvester did some mining here as well as a few blacksmiths who made the journey with pack-horses or on sleds during the winter when the river was frozen over to obtain a little of the black mineral. In the fall of 1883 I. Q. Sanborn, Civil War

[1] Colorado has more coal in reserve than any other state in the union. According to the United States Geological Survey, Colorado has enough coal resources to supply the entire world for the next six hundred years at the present rate of consumption.

veteran, discovered the Somerset and Bowie mines while prospecting for coking coal to sell to silver and gold camps for smelting purposes. He held the property in this vicinity for ten years and then abandoned his claims due to a slump in the silver market which decreased the demand for coking coal.

The government allowed the filing on coal locations in the North Fork because of its distance away from the railroad. Many ranchers took advantage of this opportunity and staked out coal ground near the present sites of Paonia, Hotchkiss, Somerset, Bowie, and Oliver only to hold their claims for a short time and then relinquish them. The year before the railroad was built, Edd Hanson got hold of the land in and around where the town of Somerset now stands. He accomplished what prior claimants had hoped to do and disposed of his claims at a goodly profit, selling out to the Utah Fuel Company, which was an affiliate of the Denver and Rio Grande Railroad at the time it was built into the valley.

Due to the efforts of J. C. Osgood, the Crystal River Railroad planned to build into the North Fork mining country from Marble. They purchased and surveyed a right-of-way which followed close to the North Fork River. Their crew started to build the grade, but shortly thereafter the company got into financial difficulties and J. C. Osgood lost control. The new management was not interested in constructing the proposed route and gave up the project.

Nevertheless, the threatened enterprise stimulated

construction of the Denver and Rio Grande extension
from Delta since the Rio Grande did not want to see
the Crystal River Railroad coming into its territory.
This, together with the booming fruit industry, live-
stock trade, and the recently purchased coal mine at
Somerset, resulted in the building of the North Fork's
first railroad. Fay R. Rockwell, who later made his
home in Paonia, was superintendent of this division
of the D. & R. G. and personally supervised construction of the road from Delta to Somerset. The train
reached Hotchkiss September 18, 1902, and that momentous date has gone down in local history as Railroad Day. There was a big demonstation of band-
playing, races, bucking horses, and, of course, speeches
to welcome the future carrier of civilization into the
North Fork. Benches were set up from which to view
the rodeo after the too-hastily built grandstand suc-
cumbed to the morning breezes. The only casualty
occurred when a bronco pitched into the open pavil-
ion and threw off its Mexican "twister" amid the
startled crowd.

Officials of the Utah Fuel Company called their
new mine Somerset after Somersetshire in England,
famous for its coal. After a postoffice was established
in a tent during 1902, the name was continued. In the
spring of 1903 the miners' tents began to be replaced
by company-owned houses, the first building completed being a saloon. The railroad reached Somerset
in the winter of 1902, but work had already been begun the previous summer.

For twenty consecutive years the Somerset mine produced close to 1,000 tons of coal a day. The output is still heavy. In contrast to most mines where the labor turnover is from forty to sixty per cent a year, the turnover in Somerset is only about three per cent. During the summer of 1936 the mine was awarded the second Joseph Holmes certificate for its record in having so few accidents in proportion to its production.

Before the iron rails of civilization entered the valley, the Juanita Coal and Coke Company opened up a mine a few miles below Somerset. It sold coal for domestic use in the North Fork until the railroad made outside markets available. After the mine came under control of Alexander Bowie, the few original shacks were transformed into an attractive village and the mine was improved into one of the best-equipped in the West. Its name was changed from Juanita to Bowie under its new management to prevent postal officials from confusing it with a town near Gunnison, a title of identical sound through spelled differently.[2]

In 1903 Charles Oliver filed on land containing the old Sylvester bank. His son, the late Clinton Oliver, started the mine running about ten years ago, and he and his sons have made an outstanding success in developing new territories for the consumption of North Fork coal. Today coal from this region is sold in numerous western states from the Missouri River to the Pacific coast.

There are also many small so-called wagon mines in

[2] Waunita Hot Springs.

the North Fork area, but their customers are chiefly among the local ranchers, and they do not attempt to sell in large commercial quantities.

One of the biggest deposits of coal in Colorado is held by Samuel G. Porter on his 3800-acre claim about six miles up Minnesota Creek from Paonia. Because of its location off the railroad and insufficient demand for the black treasure, this huge amount of concealed riches lies discovered but unexploited, awaiting only the time when an increased market will transform this pastoral retreat into a large, bustling mining town, perhaps proving the theory that the greatest potential wealth of the North Fork is in its coal resources.

PART II
PIONEER PERSONALITIES

XII
STATESMAN

STATESMAN

AT THE TURN of the century, when the morality of politics was even lower than usual, the North Fork Valley contributed a young statesman to the political wars whose name became a byword to lobbying corporations and trusts as one of the few leading representatives on Denver's capitol hill who could not be bought. If the life of this remarkable personality had not been cut short in its prime, it is the consensus of opinion among those who were acquainted with his ability and character that he would have gone far not only in state politics but in the national capitol as well. No history of the North Fork is complete without a portrayal of one of its greatest citizens—Mead Hammond, the Abraham Lincoln of Colorado.

Charles Mead Hammond was born in Bradford, Pennsylvania, but when still a boy he followed the tide of the westward movement and came with his family to the North Fork region of western Colorado soon after the Indians were removed and the country was thrown open for settlement. In the primitive surroundings of this unexploited land he spent his youth, developing along with the frontier. Like many outstanding men, Mead had the vision and courage to rise above his environment and reach for a dream.

Through self-instruction and the experiences of life, rather than from the background of a college class-room, he qualified himself for admittance to the bar. This was not easy since most of his study had to be done at night when his big muscles cried for rest after wrestling all day with the untamed, rocky soil on his father's ranch. Mead's father and three brothers were among the largest cattle operators in the North Fork, and the story is told by some that even during the round-ups Mead rode the cow-country with law books in his brush-worn saddlepockets and studied them each evening by the faint glow of the campfire.

As attorney for Paonia he was instrumental in se-curing the mountain springs from which the town derives its water supply; and he, in conjunction with Fay Rockwell, mayor of Paonia, was responsible for the construction of Paonia's municipally owned water plant. Mead's work as city attorney showed his ca-pacity for starting and successfully carrying through large projects and prepared him for rendering greater service in the state legislature.

At the age of twenty-six years Mead became a member of the People's, or Populist, party when it was formed in 1892. This party was organized to unite the wage-earners of the East with the western and southern farming elements. It was the first and last great co-operative effort of American farmers to reorientate the government in the interests of agri-culture and break the iron grip of a rising industrial-ism on the political helm. At its national convention the Populist party criticized the two major parties and built a platform favoring the free coinage of silver, a graduated income tax, government ownership of railways and telegraphs, the initiative and referendum, shorter working hours for city laborers, direct election of United States senators, restricted immigration, postal savings banks, and the Australian ballot. Eastern capitalists opposed these principles as radical and dangerous to property rights, but most of the feared planks were later enacted into law under the conservative banner of the Republican party.

In 1898 Mead Hammond was elected to the Colorado lower house on the Populist ticket, distinguishing himself by being the only victorious state official chosen on a straight Populist ticket. Those of his party associates who won did so on some sort of fusion ticket. When Mead strode into the legislature to serve his first term as representative of Delta and Montrose counties, lobbyists glanced apprehensively at the iron-jawed young lawyer. He was only thirty-two, but the struggles and hardships on the North Fork frontier had not only hardened his tall, powerful body[1] but had helped weld a character and mind which were fit to cope with the intrigues and problems that enveloped the statehouse. At this time political corruption was even more prevalent than ordinarily. Wealthy monopolists and combinations had their fingers in most of the legislation, and underhanded trades and bribery were the fashions of the day.

[1] As a test of strength Mead once lifted a three hundred pound barrel of salt into the back of a high wagon.

Mead became one of the leaders of the organization minority which under his tutelage became the majority on the sixtieth day of the session, and for the remainder of the term he was one of the recognized leaders of the House. At first some of his colleagues covertly smiled at this uneducated, uncouth giant from the Western Slope, but they soon learned to respect his unusual fund of common sense and general knowledge which he so ably exhibited in debates and discussions. His long hours of study as a boy under unfavorable conditions had developed remarkable powers of concentration which he used to good advantage while attending the notoriously noisy meetings of the lower house. He became prominent as a fighter for the principles he thought right, and his unflinching honesty and integrity won him the respect, if not the love, of all who knew him. Like all men, he made mistakes, but he remained true to his own unwritten code of right and wrong under the most severe tests.

Mead ran to succeed himself and was elected by a big majority to the Thirteenth General Assembly. His combination controlled the House during the entire term, including an extra session called by Governor Orman to correct the new general revenue law, which had been ruled against by the Colorado Supreme Court. In the regular session Mead introduced the Gunnison Tunnel Bill by which the state was to undertake construction of an artificial waterway through the mountains, taking water from the Gunnison River to irrigate the Uncompahgre country. Shortly before this momentous enterprise was presented to the legislature, C. T. Rawalt, representative of Gunnison County, who had planned to revive the old Gunnison Normal School Bill requesting an appropriation to construct a college in western Colorado, called Mead aside.

"Since both of our projects are for the Western Slope," Rawalt commented, "they may kill each other. Therefore, if you think my desired appropriation will block the success of your Gunnison Tunnel Bill, I won't ask for it."

"Would you do that for me?" Mead asked, looking down at his colleague with a quizzical smile.

"No," replied Rawalt, "but I would do so because I think that your proposal will be best for western Colorado. However, I'm not satisfied that either need be killed."

Mead laid a big hand on his friend's shoulder.

"We'll tie them together with barbed wire, and they'll either win or fall together."

Due in a large part to Mead's tireless efforts, both bills were passed—one initiating steps to bring life-producing water to lands in the Uncompahgre Valley, while the other conceived Western State College at Gunnison—the only institution in western Colorado which offers a full college course.

What Mead might have done in the way of further developing this somewhat neglected half of the state will never be known, for early in 1903 he was stricken with diabetes, dread forerunner of certain death until the recent discovery of insulin. For some time thereafter Mead stayed at Gunnison and restricted his diet to mountain trout in an effort to postpone the inevitable. During October he returned to his home at Paonia with the intention of leaving the next day for California. Starved for sweets, he insisted upon one more taste of his sister's delicious preserves which he had so often enjoyed in the past. Soon after eating the forbidden fruit he went into a coma from which he never regained consciousness. Western Colorado's great champion had left the arena.

XIII
THE LAST COWBOY

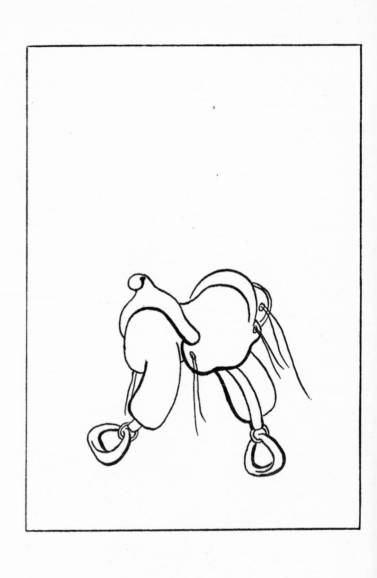

THE LAST COWBOY[1]

THE YOUNGEST and last of the early-day hard riding cowboys has thrown his brush-scarred saddle into the "Old Corral" beside the rusty riding outfits of his veteran predecessors, most of whom have long ago "jingled" their favorite cow-ponies to travel the misty trail over the Great Divide. A new type of cow-puncher now rides the cattle range—less primitive than the former denizens but not so adept at riding broncos, swinging the lasso, or handling cattle.

Tede[2] Hice, last of the old clan, was born in the San Luis Valley of Colorado in 1882. He started his brilliant career with horses and cattle as soon as he was big enough to climb on a saddle. When twelve years old he was hired as a regular cow-hand to help drive one of the first herds of cattle between Coal Mountain and Mount Gunnison on to the large Minnesota Creek range, night-herding them single-handed on his night of duty.

A large number of wild horses ran loose the year around on Green Mountain, many never having seen a man except to have branding irons clapped on them.

[1] This biography was published in *Space* two days before "the last cowboy's" death. It was read as his obituary at one of the largest funerals ever held in western Colorado. At the conclusion of the reading, a soloist sang "Take Me Back to My Boots and Saddle."
[2] Pronounced "Teed."

An enjoyable pastime of the younger cowboys was to run a bunch of these "broncs" into a corral and try to saddle and ride them while the older cow-hands and cattlemen looked on. Before he was fifteen, Tede rode with the best of these veterans as they swung their sombreros and attempted to keep contact with the ricocheting backs of the Green Mountain outlaws. The young "twister" also became a common figure at the North Fork's Fourth-of-July celebrations where he participated in the bucking contests, winning a name for himself as the best bronco-buster in western Colorado.

At one of these rodeos Tede was watching a horse-race when the leader, a big, spirited animal, suddenly began bucking and threw his jockey. The crowd watched in amazement as the youthful rider ran up to the pitching horse, grabbed the bridle-reins, and jumped on. The bucker took a few plunges with his new rider, then stretched out into a full gallop. Surprised silence grew into loud applause as the spectators leaned forward to better see the beautifully built racer pound around the track, gradually pull up on the others, and win the race by a nose.

Tede advanced from a rider to foreman of the Stirrup Bar Ranch where he won a reputation as the best roper as well as the champion tobacco chewer of the entire Western Slope of Colorado. No one ever detected a falter in the rhythmical working of his lower jaw on a quid of juicy plug whether he was riding at top-speed over rough ground after an un-

Tede Hice on Bluedog

ruly steer or feeling the jerk of a yearling when it hit
the end of his accurate rope. As captain of the round-
ups he invariably took the long end of the rides,
priding himself on being able to do more in a day's
work than any other rider. Tede remained with the
Stirrup Bar outfit for over twenty years, and his
loyalty and devotion to the "Boss" were under all cir-
cumstances typical of the old-time hands who had
passed from the western scene.

No mother had more pride and affection for her
children than Tede did for his string of cow-horses.
He was cutting out cattle on Porter, his best cow
pony, when a bull which had been fighting more or
less during the entire day's drive suddenly broke
away from an opponent and burst through the herd
with his conqueror close behind. Tede was unaware
of the charge and preparing to head a steer when he
felt his horse jump quickly to the side. Porter's timely
leap saved his rider's life but was a fraction of a second
too late to save himself. As the fleeing bull passed,
his horn gored Porter's side, and on the following day
a merciful bullet ended the life of the greatest cow-
horse Tede ever rode.

Tede's fame as a hunter and fisherman equalled his
reputation as a ranch top-hand. He began his record
before seasons and bag limits, returning triumphant
from many a chase after venison, bear, and mountain
sheep. His skill as a fisherman gave rise to the suspicion
that he could even pull mountain trout out of the
sagebrush.

One morning three years ago[3] he took down his willow-pole and started up Crystal Creek, near his cow-camp, to catch a mess of fish for dinner. It was a warm day and the clear water of the stream glistened in the sun. Tede noticed that it was uncomfortably hot as he tossed his line into a likely trout pool. Suddenly everything went black. He reeled forward, stumbling in his high-heeled boots. Laying down his pole he tried to roll a cigarette, but the tobacco kept spilling out of his trembling fingers. In a daze he turned back toward camp, a gradual paralysis gripping him.

A few days later another empty saddle was tossed into the "Old Corral" and the gate was closed.

[3] 1935.

XIV
THE TRIGGERLESS GUN

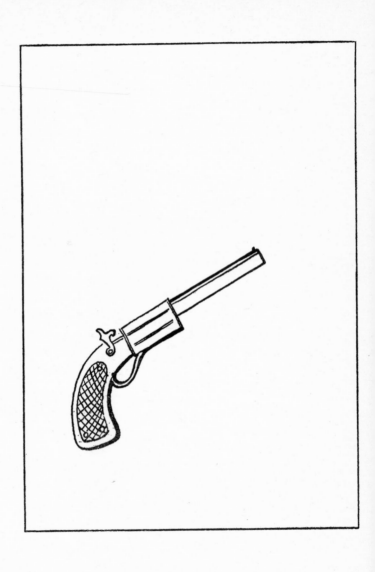

THE TRIGGERLESS GUN

JINGLING spurs and rustling *chaparejos* are still familiar to the cow-country of the North Fork, but the long round-ups and gunmen passed forever with the coming of barbed wire and civilization. There are a few old-timers who still remember the yearly rides of the eighties when loudly dressed and picturesque cowboys were the aristocrats of the region. These remaining pioners like to reminisce about dusty "punchers" squatted about campfires after the day's ride, singing, spinning yarns, and drinking sour grape wine which they often obtained when the round-up passed the farms on German Mesa. The famous Diamond Joe outfit, the Night Riders, and the wild-horse impromptu rodeos also contributed to the color of this little-known section of western Colorado, and they all played a part in the life of the notorious bad-man of the North Fork—Sam Angevine, who with his triggerless gun shot an impressive but questionable name for himself among the early settlers.

Sam Angevine originally hailed from Nova Scotia, Canada, where he had a reputation as a barroom fighter. On one occasion he received such a beating that in spite of his tall, powerful body he swore never to use his fists again. He bought a Colt six-shooter and filed away its trigger notches so that the hammer fell immediately when released by the thumb, giving him an advantage on the draw. He practiced constantly and became more accurate with a revolver than most men are with a rifle.

When the Ute Indians were removed from the North Fork to the arid plains of Utah, settlers came streaming into this newly opened country. They gazed in wonder at its fertile valleys, crystal creeks, and lofty mountains—the favorite hunting grounds of the Utes, one-time monarchs of Colorado. Sam Angevine was among the first to enter. Bad blood started when he sold the preemption claim of his neighbor, John McIntyre. They met on the big round-up, and a gun battle ensued while numerous cowpunchers stampeded their horses to get out of the line of fire. A hole in the thumb of Angevine's glove suddenly caught on the hammer of his six-shooter ending the fight, and McIntyre was taken away badly wounded.

In spite of his reputation as a dangerous man, Angevine was a pleasant and soft-spoken companion except when aroused. His vicious temper was responsible for most of his shooting frays, and he always regretted them afterwards. When a bullet from the triggerless gun cut short the life of Riley Adams over a fish-trap controversy, Angevine took a pack outfit and rode back into the hills. A posse followed him through the Minnesota and Big Muddy sections and north as far as Rawlins, Wyoming, where his trail

Aaron Clough

disappeared. A thousand dollars reward was offered for the capture of the killer, dead or alive, and his picture was posted throughout the country. Some weeks later two detectives were reading and talking about him on a Canadian train. A tall, dark-eyed man got up from a nearby seat and sauntered over to them.

"Pardon me," he interrupted, "but how'd yuh like to go back to the states?"

The detectives looked up, surprised.

"Well, let's get goin'. I'm the man you're lookin' for." At the subsequent trail an apparently intimidated jury cleared him.

Angevine's killings had a peculiar effect on his character. Naturally somewhat superstitious, he came to be haunted by the ghosts of the men he had shot. He also became suspicious that their friends and relatives were out to get him. Regardless of where he might be, he would allow no lamps to be lighted after dark for fear some enemy might take a shot at him through a window. He permitted dust to collect on the floor of his cabin to facilitate the detection of anyone who might have entered while he was away riding after cattle. If anything looked the least questionable, he threw out his flour and other food that could be poisoned. On the round-ups he rode behind the others, never letting an armed man get in back of him.

Aaron Clough, former Indian fighter and buffalo hunter, was the only living person of whom Angevine was afraid. One afternoon he met the tall, rangy cattleman walking across the road near his ranch, armed only with a big quid of chewing tobacco.

Angevine pulled his trotting horse to a stop. "Clough," he said threateningly, "I understand that you said I oughtta be hanged."

The old frontiersman looked at him quietly, then drawled, "I did." Turning slightly, he ejected a goodly portion of his tobacco juice. "And, by God, I meant it!" Angevine, without further hesitation, spurred his horse and continued on his way.

Hoping to escape his past, the notorious gunman eventually left the North Fork country, but no matter where he went his ghosts followed him. Driven to desperation, he made a final and supreme effort to find peace of mind. He turned the triggerless gun on its last victim, himself. Dead men had completed their revenge.

XV
THE THIRD HORSEMAN

THE THIRD HORSEMAN

"BETTER take the bumps a little slower, Charlie."

As he spoke, Ed Harbinson braced himself against the tottering mowing machine which threatened to roll off the rattling wagon as it jolted along over the roadless ground. It was a warm, drowsy day on the East Muddy, and the chirping of the mountain locusts kept up a continuous monotone.

Harbinson glanced back at the three horsemen— Charles Perrin, Alexander Labell, and Peter Small, who were walking their horses abreast a short distance behind the ricocheting vehicle.

"One well directed bullet could damn near clip off the three of 'em," Harbinson observed silently, secretly ashamed of himself for his nervous anxiety.

However, Tom Welch's warning dwelt heavily on his mind. He could not forget the wild look in the high-tempered Irishman's blue eyes when he had said, "This is my land, and if you cut hay on it, it will be over my dead body." This threat had not been taken seriously since Welch's only claim to the clearing was that he had cut hay on it the year before. Nevertheless, Harbinson had brought along his rifle just in case of trouble, but the rest of the hay crew had come unarmed, believing that at the worst a free-

141

for-all fist-fight would decide the jurisdiction of the park.

The disputed clearing lay just around the next bend, and Harbinson clutched his .45-.90 apprehensively as he peered into the surrounding spruce and quaking aspens to see what might lie concealed in their gloomy shadows. He imagined that the indifferent conversation of the riders became somewhat tense as the open park came into view. His piercing eyes examined the timothy field closely as they approached. The horsemen were riding closer now, and Harbinson could hear them more plainly as they talked.

Alexander Labell was speaking, and in spite of the proximity of possible danger Harbinson found himself listening intently to the quiet, well-modulated voice.

"You can always tell the color of a feller's insides by the way he dies. If he takes it smilin'—well, yuh know he's a man."

The tall grass in the small park waved gently in the breeze. Everything looked peaceable enough, but some sinister suspicion kept Harbinson constantly alert.

"Why did Labell speak of death at a time like this?" he thought. "It was a bad omen."

"Well, Ed," Perrin spoke to Harbinson, "you might as well lay down your gun. I don't even see a coyote."

The gunman did not answer. His gaze had fastened itself on a huge spruce log lying a short way ahead. He had often seen that fallen monarch of the forests, but he had never before noticed the rocks which had been chucked around it. The fragrant wild hay brushed against the horses' bellies as they were guided through the luxuriant growth.

"Good-lookin' crop," commented Charlie Majors as he clucked to the team.

As if his statement were a signal, the crack of a rifle echoed through the mountains, and a bullet spat against the mower and whirred loudly off into space.

"Run for cover!" Harbinson yelled, jumping off the wagon.

Another deafening report sounded, and Labell slumped over in his saddle. The terrified colt stampeded toward the spruce log, but a gleaming gun-barrel appeared over the side and a swishing compact of lead and horseflesh cut short his mad gallop.

Harbinson dropped down in a little sink surrounded by rocks, hugging the ground as the entire East Muddy rang with gunshots. Bullets smashed against the protecting rocks and beat a singing tattoo off the iron wheels of the mowing machine. Arthur Wade, who was riding several miles away, heard the firing and thought some hunters had run on a big herd of deer or elk.

While crouched in his hideout, Harbinson observed that the barricaded log hid the killer who was doing the most shooting. Quickly raising his gun, Harbinson sent a return projectile along the ground. As it contacted the fortified spruce, an old, dilapidated hat arose just above the bulwark. Harbinson quickly reloaded and took speedy aim at the visible hat-band. He jerked on the trigger, and the hat vanished from view.

Suddenly the resounding echoes ceased and a menacing quiet followed. Harbinson looked furtively around in expectation of a new attack. He started when a hoarse voice bawled from the encircling timber, "Take your dead and get the hell out o' here!"

Charles Majors and Ed Harbinson hesitantly raised themselves above the high grass—the lone survivors of the ambuscade. Peter Small lay mortally wounded and died the following day. Charles Perrin also was found in serious condition and died later from the effects of a splintered bullet wound. Harbinson finally discovered the third horseman, reclining face downward in the timothy. He turned Labell gently over to see if a spark of life remained. Rigor mortis had already started in the lifeless corpse.

"Hurry! Let's lift him on the wagon and get out of here," said Majors as he approached. "Why, what's the matter?"

Majors looked down on the pale, drawn countenance and felt his pulse quicken when he saw that the dead man's mouth was frozen into a ghastly but unmistakable smile! As they carried him away, Labell's last words flashed through Harbinson's mind:

"If he takes it smilin'—well, yuh know he's a man."

After Majors and Harbinson had left with their dead and wounded, Thomas Welch, Butcherknife Ed, and Welch's oldest son came out on the battleground.

There beside the decaying spruce log they found the body of sixteen-year-old Thomas Welch Jr. with a bullet through his hat-band. Welch had paid his price for the fall cutting.

XVI
DIAMOND JOE'S PROTEGE

DIAMOND JOE'S PROTEGE

IN THE mid-eighties John D. Morrissey established the Diamond Joe ⟨JO⟩ cattle ranch on Crystal Creek.[1] Although unable to read or write, the tall, muscular newcomer was proficient in two fields—blacksmithing and judging mine locations. When large deposits of lead and silver were discovered at California Gulch in 1877 and 1878, Morrissey came in with the rush. The town of Leadville[2] sprang up, and by the fall of 1879 it had grown into a city of fifteen thousand inhabitants, most of whom were engaged in mining. Morrissey started a blacksmith shop in the rapidly growing community, and while there he gained a reputation for being adept at recognizing the value of mining land.

In Leadville Morrissey became acquainted with J. C. Reynolds, short, full-bearded prospector, whose vocation before he came to Leadville during the excitement was driving a freight team from Missouri to Colorado. Like many others, Reynolds struck it rich and became a millionaire over night. His luck con-

[1] A winter camp was also started in Smith Fork Canyon below Crawford.

[2] Sometimes termed the "Cloud City" because it is situated nearly two miles above sea level.

tinued, and he became so wealthy that people began calling him Diamond Joe. His property interests expanded with his wealth, and he purchased some land outside the state, believing that it contained gold ore. Nevertheless, he sent his friend Morrissey to make a final check on it before mining operations were begun. On the return trip Morrissey had progressed only a short way when he met a wagon drawn by an ox-team and loaded with men and mining machinery.

"Where are yuh headed for?" Morrissey inquired.

"Diamond Joe sent us to start diggin' on his gold mine near here," one of the miners answered.

"Might as well throw your tools out and start back. The property is worthless." The group looked surprised but complied with Morrissey's advice, which later proved correct at someone else's expense.

This episode so won Diamond Joe's confidence and gratitude that he began relying on the blacksmith's judgment in other ventures. Morrissey was instrumental in discovering the rich Crown Prince mine for Diamond Joe at Leadville in which Morrissey was given an interest. Like so many individuals who suddenly find themselves with more money than they know what to do with, Morrissey became a prolific spender. He spent most of it gambling on horse races and usually lost. Another investment was his cattle ranch on Crystal Creek, which he named after his friend and benefactor, Diamond Joe.

The Diamond Joe cow-camp on Crystal Creek became the traditional meeting place for sixty or more

The Diamond Joe Cow-Camp

early-day cowboys of the North Fork. Here about mid-June various groups of riders, representing different sections of the North Fork cow-country, would assemble. At this time all trails led to the Diamond Joe. Numerous temporary camps sprang up around the cow-cabin, the cow-hand delegates of each outfit camping separately. Growing herds of mustangs, cow-ponies of the arriving buckaroos, were grazed nearby. Countless compfires flickered each evening under the bright western stars, throwing fantastic shadows of lean, colorfully dressed cowboys against the log sides of the lone cow-camp. The nickering of restless horses, quiet voices, and loud laughs harmonized with the plaintive-voiced serenade of coyotes to punctuate the stillness of frosty nights.

Finally at the appointed time when all the cowmen had made their appearance, a captain of the round-up was elected, and on the subsequent day camps were broken and the long summer's ride began. The purpose of the ride was to gather the cattle, brand the calves, and push the herds up on their summer ranges. The round-up worked Crystal Creek, Saddle Mountain, Mount Lamborn, upper Minnesota Creek, the Big Muddy, Holy Terror Creek, Leroux, Surface Creek at Cedaredge, and around to the point of Grand Mesa near Grand Junction.

Occasionally the wealthy mining man would visit his Crystal Creek domain. During one of the short sojourns at his cow-camp, he noticed the picture of a race horse on the open page of a newspaper lying on the floor. Picking up the sheet he examined the printing for a while, and then, with some embarrassment, asked one of the cowboys in the room to read it aloud. His natural enthusiasm for playing the ponies was aroused, and on the following day he left for Denver to see and bet on the June races.

In two or three years after the Diamond Joe came into existence, Morrissey went bankrupt. His Crystal Creek ranch was sold for taxes and came into the possession of W. J. Reed, Sam Hartman, and Ed Creighton. Although the Diamond Joe was not as permanent as the other cattle ranches of the North Fork, due to the romantic character of its founder, the unusual brand, and the picturesque rendezvous scenes around the Diamond Joe cow-camp,[3] it has became the recognized symbol of all the color of early North Fork cow-land.

[3] The old camp is still in existence and is now owned and used by the Stirrup Bar outfit.

XVII
THE CIRCLE S KID

THE CIRCLE S KID

A NEW WEST has been built on the remnants of the old. Too few of the modern generation appreciate that the early-day westerner had to give his blood so that we of the twentieth century may have the heritage of law and order. Those hardy frontiersmen who fought Indians, rustlers, and disease for the privilege of running their great herds on the contested range are a nearly vanished race, a type which never again will walk the face of America. A last remnant of the old West still breathes in a living North Fork personality—the once famous Circle S Kid, one of the pioneers and builders of the Southwest.

Harry Edwards spent the first few years of his life in the East, where his mother was employed for some time as a governess in the distinguished Vanderbilt family. While still a child, Harry moved westward with his parents in a covered wagon drawn by a team of oxen, settling near old Fort Wallace in western Kansas. At the age of ten years the restless boy ran away from home, and twenty years passed before his family heard from him again.

Harry made his way to Texas, rustling wood for a wagon train to pay his board. A year later, although only eleven years old, he started riding the range. He rode for several cow-outfits in the Southwest, including that of John S. Chisholm, cattle king and one of the great trail blazers and pioneers of the West. Chisholm was owner of the South Springs Ranch located about thirty-five miles north of Roswell on the Pecos River. He owned more cattle at the peak of his career than any other man in the United States, pasturing them over nearly half of New Mexico. In the Pecos Valley Chisholm's word was law, and hundreds of cowboys rode the plains to tend his vast herds of cattle, identified by the jingle-bob, homeliest earmark ever put on a cow. The greatest of cattle kings contributed much to western history until his reign was broken in 1892, and his extensive domains were taken from him, marking the end of the early cow-monarchs.

While he was in New Mexico, Harry became acquainted with William H. Bonney, better known as Billy the Kid, the Southwest's most notorious desperado and its last great outlaw. Bonney was the leader of a band of ruffians who gathered cattle out of the Texas Panhandle and herded them over the state line into New Mexico. Harry was also a friend of Pat Garrett—tall, melancholy Texan who was elected sheriff of Lincoln County, New Mexico, to end the wholesale rustling and cold-blooded killings of the feared outlaws.

Garrett assembled a posse and arrested the youthful Billy the Kid and several of his men after a gunfight in which two of the bandits were killed. Billy was sen-

The Circle S Kid and Wife in New Mexico

tenced to be hanged and imprisoned at Lincoln, New Mexico, pending the execution. He escaped, killed two men, and rode jauntily out of town. Pat Garrett and John W. Poe, who later succeeded Garrett as sheriff, started out after the diminutive killer with a posse of thirteen men. They finally found his hide-out at Fort Sumner where Garrett shot him down to end the infamous adventures of Billy the Kid, credited with having killed twenty-one men, a man for every year of his short life. Garrett and Poe continued their campaign against southwestern bad-men and did much to bring law and order to that wild region.

Harry Edwards grew up in those untamed surroundings where a quick trigger-finger and an accurate aim were essentials to a long life. He became an expert with a gun and rope, winning several rodeo championships with his trained lasso. For thirteen years Harry was wagon boss of the A. Straus cattle ranch between Roswell and Liberty, New Mexico. This was not an easy job since eastern New Mexico was a tough country, and it took an outstanding man to control a group of rough, independent cowpunchers. Furthermore, an efficient foreman had to be able to cope with outlaws who would as soon kill a man as change the brand on a dogie. Harry's wife, Babe, also a crack shot, saved her husband's life more than once in this bandit-infested region. The Straus brand was Circle-S and Harry came to be known to everyone in this cattleland as the Circle S Kid.

About 1906 the short, wiry, gun-scarred cow-puncher and his wife drifted into the North Fork Valley of Colorado. Twenty years later he was a participant in one of the most spectacular gunfights ever seen in the North Fork.

Ott Petersen was for a long time the best known game warden in western Colorado. He was a tall, powerfully built man, and his one squinting eye gave him a somewhat sinister expression. Although occasionally his tactics may have been rough, perhaps necessarily, Peterson did more to preserve the wild life and enforce game laws on the West Slope than any other man.

Bad blood had existed for some time between Peterson and Harry Edwards, commonly called Shorty in this region to distinguish him from another North Fork resident by the same name. Consequently, one July day when his son, Frank, informed him that Peterson was on his way up to the Edwards's sawmill on Black Mesa, Harry wasted no time in procuring a revolver. However, his wife, knowing her husband's aptitude with firearms and fearing that he might kill Peterson in case of trouble, persuaded him to leave it in the house. So, unarmed, Harry resumed his work at the sawmill. A few minutes later three state game wardens, Jack Jennings, Roy Reed, and Ott Peterson, drove up in an automobile. Peterson stepped out. Striding up to Harry he held out his hand in a friendly gesture.

"I've got papers to search this outfit," he said.

Shorty knocked down the proffered hand. "You don't need papers to search this outfit. Go ahead."

Peterson looked surprised. "All right, you don't need to shake hands with me if you don't want to, you little —— — ——."

Harry swung for Peterson's face, but his opponent's greater height was so accentuated by the higher ground on which he was standing that the smaller man's fist fell short of its mark, landing heavily on the game warden's chest. This started hostilities. Although he was much larger, Peterson found it difficult to hit the active little man who, among his varied experiences, had fought in the prize ring. Upon becoming aroused, the usually good-natured and pleasant Harry had been transformed into as ferocious appearing an individual as anyone had ever seen in the North Fork, not excluding the notorious killer, Sam Angevine.

It is no discredit to Peterson that he finally drew his .38-caliber police special from its holster to defend himself. The Circle S Kid had been raised with trouble on the western plains. He was made of the same mold and brought up in the same environment as Pat Garrett and John Poe. If he had been criminally inclined, he would have become another Billy the Kid.

Peterson himself was not a safe man to take liberties with, either, and the word fear was never registered in his vocabulary. This was the first and last time that any man ever got the best of Peterson, but this was no reflection on the warden's prowess since in this instance he was dealing with the most dangerous and versatile fighter west of the Missouri River.

"Drop that cutter," Harry ordered, "and let's fight it out man to man."

Peterson lowered his gun, evidently to comply with the request. Whatever else may be said of Peterson, his indomitable courage did not fail him even under this acid test.

"Don't lay that gun down, Ott!" Roy Reed shouted. "That fellow will chop you all to hell!"

Peterson again raised his revolver. Harry continued to approach slowly, resembling a mountain lion stalking its prey. Suddenly he threw his left hand toward Peterson's face and ducked. The warden fired, the bullet singing over Harry's head and hitting the stem of a locomotive oil can.

Harry started backward, working his way swiftly but cautiously to a nearby open shed in which lay a rifle. When he grabbed the gun, Reed and Jennings ran back out of line. Harry's family and employees at the mill stood around, anxiously watching the deadly combat.

Harry jumped behind one end of a boiler which stood in the shed while Peterson squatted down behind the other end. For the first time since he had left New Mexico the Circle S Kid was again in his element as he grasped the cold barrel of his rifle. Few gunmen would have cared to have been in Peterson's position. Billy the Kid himself would have hesitated shooting it out with so formidable a shot as the former Circle S foreman.

Dead shots, like any other type of artist, are born and not made. Harry was gifted with that remarkable co-ordination and keen sight which makes a great batter, golfer, or sharpshooter. His unerring eye had been tested in the bad-lands of the Southwest not only with a gun but with a rope. His natural ability with the "cutter" and rifle had been seasoned by more than twenty years of experience on the cattle ranges of Texas and New Mexico. This was the first time since he came to the North Fork that the Circle S Kid had been given an opportunity to exhibit his skill as a gunfighter, but his reputation had followed him from the plains country. Peterson conclusively proved the iron nerve for which he was noted when he stood his ground in the face of the deadliest rifle in Colorado.

Glancing over the protecting bulwark, Harry saw the warden's .38 show itself threateningly over the boiler. Raising his rifle he took quick aim at Peterson's gun hand, but seeing one of the mill workers over his sights, he crouched down without firing. A few seconds later he again peered over the tank, espying the top of his enemy's head. With lightning speed Harry shot, the deafening report re-echoing loudly through the hills. The bullet spat against the top of the boiler, stripping it about eighteen inches as it tore through to crease some hair off Peterson's scalp. Peterson ducked and risked two chance shots which nearly hit their mark as they whirred noisily off into space.

The clamorous explosions died away and once more quiet prevailed. The pungent aroma of burning powder filled the shed. Suddenly the unflinching Peterson raised up again as he looked over the rampart to take aim. Harry, who had been patiently awaiting some such indiscretion, whipped up his rifle and pressed the trigger just as his opponent dodged back into hiding. A cry of pain escaped the warden as the deadly missle cut through his shoulder, cleaving a suspender and a holster strap.

Slipping another cartridge into his gun, Harry started hurriedly around the boiler. Realizing the danger to Peterson's life, Frank Edwards unexpectedly caught his father from behind and wrested the rifle from his grasp.

"Stay with him, boy," Peterson said as he stepped around the big tank. His shoulder was splotched with blood. The revolver trembled slightly in his hand. Harry's wife also ran up to help hold her husband. Jennings and Reed approached, grasping their Winchesters in readiness.

"Let me loose!" Harry exclaimed, struggling to free himself.

Peterson struck him over the head, and one of the spectators jumped on his back, throwing the combatant to the ground. Two others ran over to assist in keeping him down. Harry looked up from where he lay into the muzzle of Peterson's revolver. He could see no cartridges in the cylinder. There might be one shell remaining under the hammer, but Harry was willing to take the chance.

"Pull her off, you —— ——!" he said. Turning to those holding him, he whispered, "If he lets that hammer down, turn me loose."

Peterson backed off a few steps, weak from loss of blood. One of his companions handed him a Winchester, and the three game wardens held Harry at bay as he was allowed to rise.

"If anyone has guts enough to throw me a six-shooter, I'll clean the three of 'em right here in the open!" Harry cried, getting to his feet.

"Cool off, Dad," Frank advised. "This won't get you nowhere."

"Come on along and ride down to Gunnison with us," Peterson ordered.

"Why should I ride to Gunnison with you?" Harry asked defiantly.

"I'm afraid you might shoot me in the back."

"Shut up, Ott!" Jennings snapped, "or someone will get killed. He's not afraid of you."

Finally Harry was persuaded to drive with the wardens to Gunnison to stand trial. While he was down there he told R. G. Parvin, head of the state game and fish department, "If you send Peterson up there again, I'll really get him." Peterson was ordered to stay away and never again was seen in the vicinity of Harry's sawmill.

The trial was the most spectacular ever seen in Gunnison. It lasted four days in a constantly crowded court room. Harry pleaded self-defense and was cleared.

"Some people have said that Peterson was yellow," Harry remarked after the trial. "But I don't think he was. Anyone who dared show his head over that boiler right after I creased it had to have plenty of guts." This compliment was typical of the inherent sportsmanship of the early West.

XVIII
THE LOST TRAIL

THE LOST TRAIL

AMONG the most colorful and interesting characters of the North Fork were its mountain hermits. Like the early-day cattle kings and cowboys they have passed from the present scene, carrying the undisclosed motives for their lonely sojourns to unheralded graves.

These unusual men made their appearance amid the quiet, picturesque North Fork mountains from different parts of the world. So far as it is possible to see into the heavy mists that surrounded their past lives, many of them appeared to have once been leaders of power and influence in their respective communities. They were all strong individualists of varied temperaments seeking escape from a mysterious foe. Some apparently were wealthy entrepreneurs from populous cities, hoping to discover in the opposite extreme of existence the happiness which they could not find in the society of a Park Avenue or a Wall Street. The hidden reasons for the seclusive existence of these mountaineers may be passed off as fear of the law, broken homes, or disappointments in love. While these and other factors undoubtedly played a part, the real cause of their abnormality lies in something deeper and more complex.

The majority of thinking persons either consciously or unconsciously cherish some pet ideal or desire which becomes an integral part of their lives. A famous journalist once compared this inward feeling of faith and hope to a bedraggled little man standing in a crowded streetcar. He was tired and dirty after a long day's work with pick and shovel. There was nothing of interest about the unprepossessing individual except that in one grimy hand lay a lovely, white violet which he held high above the crowd to protect the delicate petals from being crushed or tainted. This man's flower is analagous to some vision or dream which most men and women, regardless of their status on the social ladder, keep in the hidden city of their minds. It may be a belief as revered as the one for which the Christian martyrs died. It is exemplified in the faith that a mother may have for her little child or the adoration that a romantic young bride may hold for the man she marries. The proverbial violet of the human mind is fashioned in as many molds as there are different types of people.

Some realize this secret dream, but many lose the trail which leads to their goal. However, most of those who fail continue to seek for the desired bit of perfection as they journey along their rocky roads. Occasionally the long sought-after vision appears before them like a mirage of cool water on the heated desert. At first, like the inexperienced desert rat, they rush over in exultation and kneel down, only to press their dry lips on the burning sands of reality.

However, disillusionments do not long discourage most of mankind. At all costs their ideal must be preserved, for if it dies something of irreparable value will go out of their lives. They instinctively feel that it is better to nourish an unattainable dream than be entirely devoid of any thought which might flavor this earthly sphere with a little of the divine. A few never cease to seek even though hopelessly lost. Others refuse to face reality and train their brains to believe the promptings of their own or someone else's imagination. The normal mind is very elastic, and it is not difficult to pervert truth into falsehood if the process serves to make the believer feel that he is winning the primary objective of his or her life.

The lone mountaineers of the North Fork may be classified in that number who are unable to find the lost Shangri-la either in imagination or actuality. They were among that minority group who permanently lose hope and fail to protect the hidden flower of idealism. Without this guiding light, they found it impossible to long continue their march. They turned away to seek refuge from themselves and the world in the desperate but seemingly fruitless hope of finding a little contentment after the mysterious and veiled mainspring of their lives had been broken. Although their hearts had died, they continued to exist in the land of the living until a merciful fate finally brought them peace and possibly a new chance.

In the subsequent pages I shall sketch the lives of a representative group of the North Fork hermits— an admirable but tragic race of men who missed the trail.

XIX
THE RECLUSE OF HUBBARD CREEK

THE RECLUSE OF HUBBARD CREEK

REUBEN DOVE drifted into the North Fork country about 1890. Some reports were that he had come all the way from Virginia. For a time he settled on an eighty-acre farm in an isolated section about twelve miles from Hotchkiss near Leroux Creek. When Edd Hanson bought his little ranch, Dove moved even farther away from the haunts of man, establishing his unenclosed domicile under an overhanging cliff near Hubbard Creek.

In this primitive environment Dove spent the remaining thirty years of his life. He lived there in solitude the year around, trapping, hunting, fishing, and searching for wild honey. Each spring he ventured into civilization for a few days in order to sell the furs that he had assembled during the winter months. His food consisted primarily of wild meat although he raised a garden near his hermitage in which he planted tobacco and a few vegetables. During the summer and fall he collected wild dandelions and potatoes in flour sacks which he hung on surrounding trees and stumps for winter use.

Popular speculation concerning the motive underlying Dove's withdrawal from society seems to have accepted the story attributing his decision to a disappointing business transaction. In vigorous young manhood Dove is said to have grasped a normally profitable opportunity to prosper through a contract for cutting railroad ties. His quantity delivered at the trackside, he was astounded to find the contract permitted what seemed to him ruthless culling by the railroad's official inspector. Protracted, heated disagreement ended in his accepting the sum tendered in payment with, it is said, the emphatically voiced resolve never to do another day's work for any man.

The hermit of Hubbard Creek became a North Fork legend. He was a rosy-cheeked man with a Tarzan-like physique. The story is told that while following a trail he would often trudge sixty miles a day through the mountains. He made many of his own cartridges, filling discharged shells with powder and lead and using the heads of matches for priming.

Dove was a suspicious individual and greeted strangers with a gun in his hand. Although unsociable and desiring to be left alone, he was a cultured visitor if he could be inveigled into a conversation. In spite of the total absence of any feminine influence, Dove was usually neat and clean. This might be of interest to certain psychologists who have advanced the theory that without the female element man soon reverts back in appearance to his ape-like ancestors. Unlike some of his fellow hermits in other portions of the North Fork, Dove seldom did any reading. Hunting and trapping occupied most of

Reuben Dove's Hermitage

his time, and he became the greatest hunter of the lone mountaineers with the possible exception of the long-haired, buckskin-clad "Moccasin" Bill Perkins of the Crawford country.

One winter's day three friends stopped at Dove's wilderness retreat to leave some salt and vegetables. They discovered the hermit lying on his bed, which was composed of a bear skin and a few blankets, under the rocky ledge of his abode. Continuous exposure and lack of a well-balanced diet had finally broken his powerful body. He had been hovering between life and death nearly six weeks, scraping meager existence from a few sacks of dried dandelions and soft potatoes hanging nearby. From his bed he was able to reach a pile of snow and the dripping sap of a box-elder tree which had provided his only water supply. Dove died a short time after he was taken to civilization for medical care, never disclosing the real secret of his self-imposed exile from mankind.

XX
THE SCHOLAR OF NEEDLE ROCK

THE SCHOLAR OF NEEDLE ROCK

LARRY BARNARD appeared in the North Fork country during its early settlement. Unlike Dove, Barnard was quite an elderly man when he arrived. Although uncommunicative about his past, the accepted belief was that he had come from Baltimore, Maryland. On his arrival he built a cabin and planted a garden some distance back of Needle Rock.

The hermit of Needle Rock was a kindly old gentleman, and mothers were not afraid to let their children play in the hills near his mountain home. He was a small and unkempt looking individual, but in spite of his homely attire he was well educated, being particularly adept at Greek and several other languages. In his cabin he kept a portfolio of his many writings which consisted of historical, political, and philosophical essays as well as stories of nature and of his own varied experiences. No one in the North Fork saw any of his manuscripts in print, but some ventured the opinion that many of his articles and stories were being published under a nom de plume.

The hermit was a lover of nature in all its aspects and wrote sketches and legends about trees, flowers, and country scenes around Crawford. Typical of his myths was the imaginary story about the creation of the tall Needle Rock. He wrote that once in the hazy past a giant author had been striding through this region when he unexpectedly stepped into a treacherous mire. As he went down to his death in the quicksand, he threw up his hand with which he had composed so many inspired works. This hand had gradually petrified into the present Needle Rock as a perpetual monument to a great writer.

The accepted motive for the hermit's retirement was unrequited love although it was also said that he had come West to make his fortune at mining and was ashamed to return home a failure. Only occasionally did he ever disclose anything which had to do with the mystery of his former life.

"You know," he once remarked to a passerby as they reclined under a tall, gnarled cedar tree gazing at the brilliant red glow of a North Fork sunset, "the apparently unimportant events of life, overlooked by most people, such as that colored sky up there are oftentimes the most beautiful and significant."

The listener remained silent, not grasping the full meaning of the hermit's words. A cool evening breeze began blowing down from the mountains. Needle Rock stood imposingly before them against the crimson background of the heavens, resembling a giant hand more than ever in the twilight. It was a time conducive to confidences.

The quiet, cultured voice continued with an imperceptible bitterness. "If I had known that simple philosophy some years ago, I wouldn't be here today —a lost soul in the wilderness."

The traveler turned and looked with interest at the speaker. The hermit was looking steadily on the sunset as though his eyes penetrated the distance and peered into antiquity. As if what he saw could not be expressed by mere words, he said no more. The inscrutable curtain that concealed his past had again fallen into place as the little scholar lost himself in silent reverie—a common habit which carries both blessing and pain to men who have lost their heritage.

XXI
HIDDEN ENEMY

HIDDEN ENEMY

THE MOST surly and dangerous of the North Fork hermits was a sullen giant who lived on a small open flat just below Soap Creek Mesa. He stood at least six feet four inches and was of magnificent proportions. His amazing feats of strength became local traditions, and there were few men who cared to cross paths with the gloomy Samson.

The recluse called himself Peter Fox, but this was undoubtedly an assumed name. During the winter months he disappeared, but each spring he returned, pulling his provisions and supplies on a sled or small cart. In addition, he often carried over his broad shoulders a heavy keg of large sixty-penny spikes, which he bore as easily as an ordinary man handles a small sack of flour.

Unlike Dove, who was a great hunter, Fox spent most of his time working on his ranch, which he had taken up under the old pre-emption act. He built a mile of fence around his claim, felling and peeling quaking aspens, which he nailed to posts with his long sixty-penny nails. He carried all the poles and posts from a hundred yards to a quarter of a mile, scorning the aid of a team. After fencing in his little farm, he built a cabin, cleared off the land,

and planted a garden. One year he raised hay, but when he was not offered an acceptable price, he burned his shocks to the ground.

Fox was always on the look-out for some unknown enemy and trusted no man. In spite of his powerful physique and ferocious temperament he gave the impression of one afraid. He appeared constantly on the alert for some relentless enemy. The rumor was whispered through the North Fork grapevine that the hermit was a member of some occult European organization which was searching for him.

One afternoon when a group of cowboys were jogging along the trail which wound by the hermitage, they saw a coyote in front of the lone cabin. One of the cowpunchers swung from his horse and took a shot at the animal. Fox, who had been standing near his door watching them, rushed into the cabin and immediately re-appeared holding an old muzzle-loading Harper Ferry's musket. Raising it in the air toward the riders, he fired. What the antique lacked in accuracy and power it made up for in noise and powder. As the thunderous report echoed through the mountains, quantities of discolored black smoke poured from the barrel. Not wishing to cause any more disturbance, the startled cow-hands moved quietly along on their way.

Fox became notorious for his hatred of mankind. Once while he was working on a country road near Curecanti Creek for Bill Irwin, the only man who was ever known to like Fox, Sam Hartman rode up.

Pulling his big, spirited cow-horse to a stop, the cat-tleman visited with Irwin for some time. However, even though Sam was facing Fox during the entire conversation, the morose hermit did not glance up from his work to speak to the cow-king.

One day some cowpunchers had gathered a herd of cattle near the giant's abode and were getting ready to build a branding fire when the suggestion was made that somebody go up to Fox's cabin and borrow an ax and a pail of water. There was considerable hesitation since none of them particularly cared about paying a call on the unfriendly hermit. Finally after some discussion Clyde McMillan, one-time champion bronco rider of western Colorado, volunteered to obtain the desired commodities.[1]

There were no tracks around the cabin; so the cowboy assumed that Fox had been away for several months on one of his mysterious missions. The door was locked, but through its panel Clyde could see a key in the inside key-hole. The cabin was filled with noisy swarms of flies, and the strong aroma of spoiled meat filled the air.

"The old boy must've left some venison lying around," Clyde thought as he reached through the broken pane for the key. However, his stretching fingers could not quite grasp the object.

"Hey," he yelled to his friends who were watching

[1] The following story of the discovery of Fox was told me by Clyde McMillan.

him expectantly. "There ain't nobody here. Come on up."

One of them ventured over. Sticking a long arm through the narrow opening he unlocked the door, threw it open, and peered inside. There lying on his bed with a blanket thrown over him lay the partly decomposed body of Fox. Lifting back the quilt the cowboys discovered a bullet hole in the hermit's head and another in his back.[2] The murderer had apparently shot Fox while he was working outside the cabin, carried him to his bed, and departed, locking the door from the outside through the panel. After the inquest, which took place several days later, the hermit was buried near his little cabin where he still lies.

The weird and strange enigmas of Fox's life and death were never solved. Possibly the hermit's legendary adversary had finally found his hide-out. On the other hand, people are seldom struck by the misfortune that they most fear. At any rate, in death the lone wolf of Soap Mesa had at last escaped from his greatest and most persistent foe—his own mental suspicions and torment.

---

[2] John Wise, one of the cowboys present when Fox was found, gives a somewhat different version. According to his account the body was so decomposed that no wound was discovered. This might lead to the possible conclusion that Fox had died from a stroke.

XXII
CURECANTI HOSPITALITY

.

CURECANTI HOSPITALITY

BILL IRWIN filed on a little flat near Curecanti Creek within a short distance of where the creek is crossed by the Black Mesa highway. He lived there for over twenty years although during the winter the snow averaged three feet and the thermometer sank to a consistent level of thirty-five or forty degrees below zero.

One of the chief characteristics of Irwin was his love for animals and birds. He was strictly a vegetarian, and no one ever knew of his killing wild life of any kind. In the winter he customarily fed flocks of grouse or other game, and he never allowed anyone to hunt on his land. He usually wintered thirty or forty head of saddle horses on his unfenced premises, feeding them native and timothy hay, which he cut in the late summer. During the warm months they ran loose on the open range. When the hermit traveled anywhere, he rode horseback or hitched up a couple of his wild mustangs to a two-wheeled cart. Occasionally the broncos would run away with him and break up his cart, but, undisturbed, Irwin would make the necessary repairs and continue nonchalantly on his way. On cold winter mornings the kind-hearted recluse would often warm up frozen water and take it out to his horses before he prepared his own breakfast. The hermit also owned numerous dogs which lived with him in his cabin, giving his home the aroma of a dog kennel.

Irwin was an entirely different type of man than his friend Fox. Although he thrived on solitude, he was very hospitable, and passing cowboys would often stop in to see him, certain of a welcome reception. He was a registered pharmacist and a graduate in chemistry. For some years he was employed by the government as a weather expert. The postoffice and trading center nearest him was Sapinero, and on his occasional visits to that hamlet he would send out his weather reports. Irwin was a great reader of all kinds of literature and kept himself well informed on national and world affairs. On his return trips from Sapinero his rickety little cart was invariably well stocked with as many magazines, newspapers, and books as it could carry.

The hermit of Curecanti Creek was a tall, muscular blond. He gained an enviable reputation in the region as a man of remarkable courage and unquestionable honesty. His hospitality, pleasant manner, and unusual intelligence won him the respect and friendship of all who knew him. He was one of those gifted individuals who is at ease in any kind of company. Sometimes he visited the neighboring cowcamps on Curecanti and Crystal creeks and helped the cowboys cut wild hay. This in no way injured his popularity with the cow-men. Irwin was the only

person who ever won the friendship of the giant of
Soap Creek Mesa.

North Fork residents often wondered why such an
outstanding and well-liked man should prefer the
company of dogs and horses to the society of men
and women. Many motives were circulated, including a broken home, disgust for the foolish com-
plexities and conventionalities of mankind, and his
high regard for the simple life and beauties of nature. However, the real secret lies buried with Irwin
in his last and permanent hermitage.

The four hermits whose misty lives I have briefly
sketched are good representatives of the other lone-
men who have roamed the North Fork in a final
search for the lost fountain of happiness. It will
never be known whether any of them found the
tranquility for which they sought. Possibly a few
discovered the right trail in their long and unknown
quests through the lofty North Fork mountains. If
they did, they may have found to their surprise that
the spark of life for which they had so long searched
in vain lay not so much in some unattainable desire
as in certain qualities within themselves, namely,
peace and freedom of mind—bearing out the statement of a great philosopher who stressed the same
belief in a slightly different way when he said, "The
kingdom of heaven lies within you."

APPENDIX

APPENDIX

TREATY NEGOTIATED WITHE THE UTES FOR
SAN LUIS VALLEY IN 1868[1]

ARTICLES of a treaty and agreement made and entered into at Washington, D. C., on the second of March, 1868, by and between Nathaniel G. Taylor, Commissioner of Indian Affairs; Alexander C. Hunt, Governor of Colorado Territory and ex-officio Superintendent of Indian Affairs, and Kit Carson, duly authorized to represent the United States, of the one part, and the representatives of the Tabewatch, Mouache, Capote, Weemunuche, Yampa, Grand River and Uintah bands of Ute Indians (whose names are hereto subscribed), duly authorized and empowered to act for the body of the people of said bands, of the other part, witness:

Article 2. The United States agree that the following district of country, to-wit: Commencing at that point on the southern boundary line of the Territory of Colorado where the meridian of longitude 107 degrees west of Greenwich crosses the same, running thence north with said meridian to a point fifteen miles due north with said meridian to a point fifteen miles due north of where said meridian intersects the 40th parallel of north latitude; thence due west to the western boundary line of said Territory; thence south with said western boundary line of said Territory to the southern boundary line of said Territory; thence east with said southern boundary line to the place of beginning, shall be, and the same is hereby, set apart for the absolute and undisturbed use and occupation of the Indians herein named and for such other friendly tribes or individual Indians as from time to time they may be willing, with the consent of the United States, to admit among them; and the United States now solemnly agree that no persons, except those herein authorized so to do, and except such

[1] *Senate Documents,* Volume II, p. 990.

officers, agents, and employees of the Government as may be authorized to enter upon Indian reservations in discharge of duties enjoined by law, shall ever be permitted to pass over, settle upon, or reside in the Territory described in this article except as herein otherwise provided.

Article 3. It is further agreed by the Indians, parties hereto, that henceforth they will and do hereby relinquish all claims and rights in and to any portion of the United States or Territories, except such as are embraced in the limits defined in the preceding article.

Article 4. The United States agree to establish two agencies on the reservation provided for in article 2, one for the Grand River, Yampa and Uintah bands, on White River, and the other for the Tabewatch, Mouache, Weeminuche and Capote bands, on Los Pinos Creek on the reservation, and at its own proper expense to construct at each of said agencies a warehouse or storeroom for the use of the agent in storing goods belonging to the Indians, to cost not exceeding fifteen hundred dollars; an agency building for the residence of the agent, to cost not exceeding three thousand dollars, and four other buildings for a carpenter, farmer, blacksmith and miller, each to cost not exceeding two thousand dollars; also a school house or mission building, so soon as a sufficient number of children can be induced by the agent to attend school, which shall not cost exceeding five thousand dollars.

The United States agree, further, to cause to be erected on said reservation, and near to each agency herein authorized, respectively, a good waterpower sawmill, with a grist mill and a shingle mill attached, the same to cost not exceeding eight thousand dollars each; provided, the same shall not be erected until such time as the Secretary of the Interior may think it necessary to the wants of the Indians.

Article 5. The United States agree that the agents for said Indians, in the future, shall make their homes at the agency buildings; that they shall reside among the Indians, and keep an office open at all times for the purpose of prompt and diligent inquiry into such matters of complaint by and against the Indians as may be presented for investigation under the provisions of their treaty stipulations, as also for the faithful discharge of other duties enjoined on them by law. In all cases of depredation on person or property they shall cause the evidence to be taken in writing and forwarded, together with their findings, to the Commissioner of Indian Affairs, whose decision, subject to the revision of the Secretary of the Interior, shall be binding on the parties to this treaty.

Article 6. If bad men among the whites or among other people, subject to the authority of the United States, shall commit any wrong upon the person or property of the Indians, the United States will, upon proof made to the agent and forwarded to the Commissioner of Indian affairs at Washington, proceed at once to cause the offender to be arrested and punished according to the laws of the United States, and also reimburse the injured person for the loss sustained.

If bad men among the Indians shall commit a wrong or depredation upon the person or property of any one, white, black or Indian, subject to the authority of the United States and at peace therewith, the tribes herein named solemnly agree that they will, on proof made to their agent and notice to him, deliver up the wrongdoer to the United States, to be tried and punished according to its laws, and in case they wilfully refuse so to do, the person injured shall be reimbursed for his loss from the annuities or other moneys due, or to become due to them, under this or other treaties made with the United States.

Article 7. If any individual belonging to said tribe of Indians or legally incorporated with them, being the head of a family, shall desire to commence farming, he shall have the privilege to select, in the presence and with the assistance of the agent then in charge, by metes and bounds, a tract of land within said reservation not exceeding one hundred and sixty acres in extent, which tract, when so selected, certified and recorded in the land book, as herein directed, shall cease to be held in common, but the same may be occupied and held in exclusive possession of the person selecting it and his family so long as he or they may continue to cultivate it. Any person over eighteen years of age, not being the head of a family, may, in like manner, select and cause to be certified to him or her for purposes of cultivation, a quantity of land not exceeding eighty acres in extent, and thereupon be entitled to the exclusive possession of the same as above directed.

For each tract of land so selected a certificate containing a description thereof and in the name of the person selecting it, with a certificate endorsed thereon that the same has been recorded, shall be delivered to the party entitled to it, by the agent, after the same shall have been recorded by him in a book to be kept in his office, subject to inspection, which said book shall be known as the "Ute Land Book."

The President may at any time order a survey of the reservation; and when so surveyed Congress shall provide for protecting the rights of such Indian settlers in their improvements, and may fix the character of the title held by each.

The United States may pass such laws on the subject of alienation and descent of property, and on all subjects connected with the government of the Indians on said reservation and the internal policies thereof, as may be thought proper.

Article 8. In order to insure the civilization of the bands entering into this treaty, the necessity of education is admitted, especially by such of them as are or may be engaged in either pastoral, agricultural or other peaceful pursuits of civilized life on said reservation, and they therefore pledge themselves to induce their children, male and female, between the ages of seven and eighteen years, to attend school; and it is hereby made the duty of the agent for said Indians to see that this stipulation is complied with to the greatest possible extent; and the United States agree that for every thirty children between said ages who can be induced to attend school a house shall be provided, and a teacher competent to teach the elementary branches of an English education shall be furnished, who will reside among said Indians, and faithfully discharge his or her duties as teacher, the provisions of this article to continue for not less than twenty years.

Article 9. When the head of a family or lodge shall have selected lands, and received his certificate as above described, and the agent shall be satisfied that he intends, in good faith, to commence cultivating the soil for a living, he shall be entitled to receive seeds and agricultural implements for the first year not exceeding in value one hundred dollars, and for each succeeding year he shall continue to farm, for a period of three years more, be shall be entitled to receive seeds and implements as aforesaid, not exceeding in value fifty dollars; and it is further stipulated that such persons as commence farming shall receive instructions from the farmer herein provided for; and it is further stipulated that an additional blacksmith to the one provided for in the treaty of October 7th, 1863, referred to in article 1 of this treaty, shall be provided with such iron, steel and other material as may be needed for the Uintah, Yampa and Grand River agency, known as the White River agency.

Article 10. At any time after ten years from the making of this treaty, the United States shall have the privilege of withdrawing the farmers, blacksmiths, carpenters and millers herein, and in the treaty of October 7th, 1863, referred to in article 1 of this treaty, provided for, but in case of such withdrawal, an additional sum thereafter of ten thousand dollars per annum shall be devoted to the education of said Indians, and the Commissioner of Indian Affairs shall, upon careful inquiry into their condition, make such rules and regulations, subject to the approval of the Secretary of the Interior, for the expenditure of said sum as will best promote the educational and moral improvement of said Indians.

Article 11. That a sum, sufficient in the discretion of Congress, for the absolute wants of said Indians, but not to exceed thirty thousand dollars per annum, for thirty years, shall be expended, under the direction of the Secretary of the Interior, for clothing, blankets and such other articles of utility as he may think proper and necessary upon full official reports of the condition and wants of said Indians.

Article 12. That an additional sum, sufficient in the discretion of Congress (but not to exceed thirty thousand dollars per annum), to supply the wants of said Indians for food, shall be annually expended under the direction of the Secretary of the Interior, in supplying said Indians with beef, mutton, wheat, flour, beans and potatoes, until such time as said Indians shall be found to be capable of sustaining themselves.

Article 13. That for the purpose of inducing said Indians to adopt habits of civilized life and become self-sustaining, the sum of forty-five thousand dollars, for the first year, shall be expended, under the direction of the Secretary of the Interior, in providing each lodge or head of a family in said confederated bands with one gentle American cow, as distinguished from the ordinary or Mexican or Texas breed, and five head of sheep.

Article 14. The said confederated bands agree that whensoever, in the opinion of the President of the United States, the public interest may require it, that all roads, highways and railroads, authorized by law, shall have the right of way through the reservations herein designated.

Article 15. The United States hereby agree to furnish the Indians the teachers, carpenters, millers, farmers and blacksmiths, as herein contemplated, and that such appropriations shall be made from time to time, on the estimates of the Secretary of the Interior, as will be sufficient to employ such persons.

Article 16. No treaty for the cession of any portion or part of the reservation herein described, which may be held in common, shall be of any validity or force as against the said Indians, unless executed and signed by at least three-fourths of all the adult male Indians occupying or interested in the same; and no cession by the tribe shall be understood or construed in such manner as to deprive, without his consent, any individual member of the tribe of his right to any tract of land selected by him, as provided in article 7 of this treaty.

Article 17. All appropriations now made, or to be hereafter made, as well as goods and stock due these Indians under existing treaties, shall apply as if this treaty had not been made, and be divided proportionately among the seven bands named in this treaty, as also shall all annuities and allowances hereafter to be made; provided, that if any chief of either of the confederated bands make war against the people of the United States or in any manner violate this treaty in any essential part, said chief shall forfeit his position as chief and all rights to any of the benefits of this treaty; but further provided, any Indian of any of these confederated bands who shall remain at peace and abide by the terms of this treaty in all its essentials shall be entitled to its benefits and provisions, notwithstanding his particular chief and band may have forfeited their rights thereto.

TREATY NEGOTIATED WITH THE UTES[1] 1873

ARTICLES of convention, made and entered into at the Los Pinos agency for the Ute Indians, on the 13th day of September, 1873, by and between Felix R. Brunot, commissioner in behalf of the United States, and the chiefs, head men and men of the Uncompahgre, Tabequache, Mouache, Capote, Weeminuche, Yampa, Grand River and Uintah bands of Ute Indians, witnesseth:

[1] *Senate Documents,* Volume I, p. 151.

Article 1. The confederated band of the Ute Nation hereby relinquish to the United States all right, title and claim, and interest in and to the following described portion of the reservation heretofore conveyed to them by the United States, viz.: Beginning at a point on the eastern boundary of said reservation, fifteen miles due north of the southern boundary of the Territory of Colorado, and running thence west on a line parallel to the said southern boundary to a point on said line twenty miles due east of the western boundary of Colorado Territory; thence north by a line parallel with the western boundary to a point ten miles north of the point where said line intersects the 38th parallel of north latitude; thence east to the eastern boundary of the Ute reservation, and thence south along said boundary to the place of beginning; provided, that if any part of the Uncompahgre Park shall be found to extend south of the north line of said described property, the same is not intended to be included therein, and is hereby reserved and retained as a portion of the Ute reservation.

Article 2. The United States shall permit the Ute Indians to hunt upon said lands so long as the game lasts and the Indians are at peace with the white people.

Article 3. The United States agrees to set apart and hold as a perpetual trust for the Ute Indians a sum of money, or its equivalent in bonds, which shall be sufficient to produce the sum of twenty-five thousand dollars ($25,000) per annum, which sum of twenty-five thousand dollars ($25,000) per annum shall be disbursed or invested at the discretion of the President, or as he may direct, for the use and benefit of the Ute Indians, annually forever.

Article 4. The United States agrees, so soon as the President may deem it necessary or expedient, to erect proper buildings and establish an agency for the Weeminuche, Mouache and Capote bands of Ute Indians at some suitable point to be hereafter selected, on the southern part of the Ute reservation.

Article 5. All the provisions of the treaty of 1868, not altered by this agreement, shall continue in force, and the following words from article 2 of said treaty, viz.:

"The United States now solemnly agrees that no persons, except those herein authorized to enter upon Indian reservations in discharge of duties enjoined by law, shall ever be permitted to pass over, settle upon or reside in the territory described in this article, except as herein otherwise provided," are hereby expressly reaffirmed, except so far as they applied to the country herein relinquished.

Article 6. In consideration of the services of Ouray, head chief of the Ute Nation, he shall receive a salary of one thousand dollars ($1,000.00) per annum for the term of ten years, or so long as he shall remain head chief of the Utes, and at peace with the people of the United States.

Article 7. This agreement is subject to ratification or rejection by the Congress of the United States and of the President.

THIRD TREATY WITH THE UTES—1880 [1]

THE CHIEFS and head men of the confederated bands of the Utes now present in Washington hereby promise and agree to procure the surrender to the United States, for trial and punishment, if found guilty, of those members of their nation, not yet in the custody of the United States, who were implicated in the murder of United States Indian Agent N. C. Meeker, and the murder of and outrages upon the employees of the White River Agency on the twenty-ninth day of September, eighteen hundred and seventy-nine, and in case they do not themselves succeed in apprehending the said parties, presumably guilty of the above mentioned crime, that they will not in any manner obstruct, but faithfully aid, any officers of the United States, directed by the proper authorities, to apprehend such presumably guilty parties.

The said chiefs and head men of the confederated bands of Utes also agree and promise to use their best endeavors with their people to procure their consent to cede to the United States all the territory of the present Ute reservation in Colorado, except as hereinafter provided for their settlement.

The Southern Utes agree to remove to and settle upon the unoccupied agricultural lands on the La Plata River, in Colorado; and if there should not be a sufficiency of such lands on the La Plata River and its vicinity in Colorado, then upon such unoccupied agricultural lands as may be found in that vicinity and in the Territory of Utah.

[1] *Senate Documents,* Volume I, pp. 181, 182, 183.

The Uncompahgre Utes agree to remove to and settle upon agricultural lands on Grand River, near the mouth of Gunnison River, in Colorado, if a sufficient quantity of agricultural land shall be found there; if not, then upon such other unoccupied agricultural lands as may be found in that vicinity and in the Territory of Utah.

The White River Utes agree to remove to and settle upon agricultural lands on the Uintah reservation in Utah.

Allotments in severalty of said lands shall be made as follows:

To each head of a family one quarter of a section, with an additional quantity of grazing land not exceeding one-quarter of a section.

To each single person over eighteen years of age one-eighth of a section, with an additional quantity of grazing land not exceeding one-eighth of a section.

To each orphan child under eighteen years of age one-eighth of a section, with an additional quantity of grazing land not exceeding one-eighth of a section; and to each other person, under eighteen years of age, now living, or who may be born prior to said allotments, one-eighth of a section, with a like quantity of grazing land.

All allotments to be made with the advice of the commission hereinafter provided, upon the selection of the Indians, heads of families selecting for their minor children, and the agents making the allotment for each orphan child.

The said chiefs and head men of the confederated bands of Utes further promise that they will not obstruct or in any wise interfere with travel upon any of the highways now open or hereafter to be opened by lawful authority in or upon any of the lands to be set apart for their use by virtue of this agreement.

The said chiefs and head men of the confederated bands of Utes promise to obtain the consent of their people to the cession of the territory of their reservation as above on the following express conditions:

First: That the Government of the United States cause the lands so set apart to be properly surveyed and to be divided among the said Indians in severalty in the proportion hereinbefore mentioned, and to issue patents in fee simple to them respectively therefor, so soon as the necessary laws are passed by Congress.

The title to be acquired by the Indians shall not be subject to alienation, lease, or incumbrance, either by voluntary conveyance of the grantee or by the judgment, order or decree of any court, or subject to taxation of any character, but shall be and remain inalienable and not subject to taxation for the period of twenty-five years, and until such time thereafter as the President of the United States may see fit to remove the restriction which shall be incorporated in the patents when issued, and any contract made prior to the removal of such restriction shall be void.

Second: That so soon as the consent of the several tribes of the Ute Nation shall have been obtained to the provisions of this agreement, the President of the United States shall cause to be distributed among them in cash the sum of sixty thousand dollars of annuities now due and provided for, and so much more as Congress may appropriate for that purpose; and that a commission shall be sent to superintend the removal and settlement of the Utes, and to see that they are well provided with agricultural and pastoral lands sufficient for their future support, and upon such settlement being duly effected that they are furnished with horses, wagons, agricultural implements, and stock cattle sufficient for their reasonable wants, and also such saw and grist mills as may be necessary to enable them to commence farming operations, and that the money to be appropriated by Congress for that purpose shall be apportioned among the different bands of Utes in the following manner: One-third to those who settle on the La Plata River and vicinity, and one-sixth to those settling on the Uintah reservation.

Third: That in consideration of the cession of territory to be made by the said confederated bands of the Ute Nation, the United States, in addition to the annuities and sums for provisions and clothing stipulated and provided for in existing treaties and laws, agrees to set apart and hold, as a perpetual trust for the said Ute Indians, a sum of money or its equivalent in bonds of the United States, which shall be sufficient to produce the sum of fifty thousand dollars per annum, which sum of fifty thousand dollars shall be distributed per capita to them annually forever.

Fourth: That as soon as the President of the United States may deem it necessary or expedient, the agencies for the Uncompahgre and Southern Utes be removed to and established at suitable points, to be hereafter selected, upon the lands to be set apart, and to aid in the support of said Utes until such time as they shall be able to support themselves, and that in the meantime the United States Government will establish and maintain schools in the settlements of the Utes, and make all necessary provision for the education of their children.

Fifth: All provisions of the treaty of March second, eighteen hundred and sixty-eight, and the act of Congress approved April twenty-ninth, eighteen hundred and seventy-four, not altered by this agreement, shall continue in force, and the following words from article three of said act, namely, "The United States agrees to set apart and hold, as a perpetual trust for the Ute Indians, a sum of money or its equivalent in bonds, which shall be sufficient to produce the sum of twenty-five thousand dollars per annum, which sum of twenty-five thousand dollars per annum shall be disbursed or invested at the discretion of the President, or as he may direct, for the use and benefit of the Ute Indians forever," are hereby expressly reaffirmed.

Sixth: That the commissioners above mentioned shall ascertain what improvements have been made by any member or members of the Ute Nation upon any part of the reservation in Colorado to be ceded to the United States as above, and that payment in cash shall be made to the individuals having made and owning such improvements upon a fair and liberal valuation of the same by the said commission, taking into consideration the labor bestowed upon the land.

Done at the city of Washington this sixth day of March, Anno Domini eighteen hundred and eighty.

BIBLIOGRAPHY

BIBLIOGRAPHY

I. BOOKS

Adams, James Truslow, *The Epic of America,* Little, Brown, and Company, Boston, 1934.

Account of an Expedition from Pittsburgh to the Rocky Mountains under command of Major S. H. Long, compiled by Edwin James from notes of Major Long, Volume II, p. 361, H. C. Carey and Lea, Philadelphia, 1823.

Baker, James N., and Hafen, Leroy R., *History of Colorado,* Volume I, Linderman Company, Inc., Denver, 1927.

Bancroft, H. H., *History of Utah (1540-1886),* The History Company, San Francisco, 1889.

Beckwith, Lieutenant E. G., *Reports of Explorations and Surveys,* Volume II, "Report of Exploration For a Route for the Pacific Railroad by Captain J. W. Gunnison," Beverly Tucker, Printer, Washington, D. C., 1855.

Bolton, H., and Marshall, T. M., *The Colonization of North America (1492-1783),* the Macmillan Company, New York, 1921.

Carhart, Arthur H., *Colorado,* Coward-McCann, Inc., New York, 1932.

Chapman, Arthur, *The Story of Colorado,* Rand McNally and Company, Chicago, 1924.

Hall, Frank, *History of Colorado,* Volume IV, The Blakelly Printing Company, Chicago, 1895.

Harris, W. R. *The Catholic Church in Utah (1776-1909),* Intermountain Catholic Press, Salt Lake City, 1909. (Escalante's journal.)

Jocknick, Sidney, *Early Days of the Western Slope of Colorado,* The Carson-Harper Company, Denver, 1913.

Paxson, Frederic L., *Recent History of the United States,* Houghton Mifflin Company, New York, 1937.

Rankin, M. Wilson, *Reminiscences of Frontier Days,* W. F. Robinson Publishing Company, Denver, Colorado, 1935.

Rippy, Fred, *Historical Evolution of Hispanic America,* F. S. Crofts and Company, New York, 1933.

II. *DOCUMENTS OF THE UNITED STATES GOVERNMENT*

House Documents, 431 House Document, Volume 92, p. 271, 57th Congress, 2nd session of 1902-1903, A Letter from Hon. James Madison, Secretary of State, to Robert R. Livingston, January 31, 1804, "With respect to the western extent of the Louisiana Purchase."

Senate Documents, Volume II, p. 990, (1st) Treaty Negotiated with the Utes for San Luis Valley in 1868.

Senate Documents, Volume I, p. 151, (2nd) Treaty Negotiated with the Ute Indians, 1873, compiled and edited by Charles J. Kappler, Government Printing Office, Washington, D. C., 1904.

Senate Documents, Volume I, pp. 181, 182, 183, (3rd) Treaty Negotiated with the Ute Indians, 1880, compiled and edited by Charles J. Kappler, Government Printing Office, Washington, D. C., 1904.

U. S. Statutes at Large, Volume 9, p. 446, "An act (by 31st Congress on September 9, 1850) proposing to the state of Texas the establishment of her northern and western boundaries, etc.", Little, Brown and Company, Boston, 1854.

U. S. Statutes at Large, Volume 9, p. 922-943, Little, Brown and Company, Boston, 1854.

III. *INTERVIEWS*

Craig, Arthur L. (Paonia), Editor of *The Paonian.*

Curtis, Horace (Paonia), Pioneer North Fork fruit grower.

Duke, Ed (Hotchkiss), Prominent North Fork pioneer, and canal builder.

Edwards, Harry (Hotchkiss), Early-day cowboy.

Fluke, Reuben (Paonia), One of the first settlers in Crawford.

Goodenow, Mrs. Albert (Paonia), One of the first settlers in Paonia.

Hammond, Fred (Paonia), Pioneer North Fork cattleman.

Hammond, Weldon (Paonia), Pioneer North Fork cattleman.

Hartman, Samuel (deceased), Early-day North Fork cattle king.

Hice, Tede (deceased), One of the last of the early-day North Fork cowboys.

Hotchkiss, Clair (Hotchkiss), Son of Enos Hotchkiss, founder of Hotchkiss.

Hunton, Mrs. George (Somerset), One of the first settlers in Somerset.

Kremling, Paul, Founder of the first Maher postoffice and former partner of Mrs. Ong, builder of first store in Crawford.

Lambertson, Frank (Paonia), a pioneer sawmill builder of the North Fork.

McMillan, Clyde (Hotchkiss), Early-day North Fork cowboy and bronco-buster.

Porter, Sam (Paonia), North Fork coal mining and water expert.

Rawalt, C. T. (Paonia), Founder of *The Paonia Newspaper.*

Sanborn, I. Q. (Somerset), Son of the first settler in Somerset, I. Q. Sanborn I.

Sanderson, Mrs. Oscar (Crawford), Crawford pioneer woman.

Short, Mr. and Mrs. Frank (Paonia), North Fork pioneers, daughter and son-in-law of I. Q. Sanborn I.

Wade, Arthur (Paonia), Son of Samuel Wade, founder of Paonia.

Wade, Frank (Paonia), Son of Samuel Wade, founder of Paonia.

Yoakum, Jessie (Paonia), First school teacher of Paonia.

IV. MISCELLANEOUS

Cafran, J. W. G., Letter addressed to A. B. Johnston of Gunnison, Colorado, November 12, 1885, from Portland, Oregon. Contains sketch of life of Captain J. W. Gunnison. (State Historical Society of Colorado.)

Greer, Taylor B., Speech, "History of the Western Slope," given at Delta County Pioneers' Picnic at Paonia, July, 1936.

Hotchkiss, Clair, Original manuscript on the early history of Hotchkiss. In the possession of Clair Hotchkiss.

Plake, John, "Exodus of the Utes," original manuscript, 1922. In the possession of the State Historical Society of Colorado.

Notes of Miss Jessie Yoakum (Manuscript), 1921, Pioneer schoolteacher at Paonia. In the possession of the State Historical Society of Colorado.

V. PAMPHLETS

Fish, H. R., *Souvenir North Fork Valley,* published by the *Paonia Newspaper,* 1905.

Shaw, Luella, *True History of Some of the Pioneers of Colorado,* Carson-Harper Company, Denver, 1909.

Wallace, H. A. (Secretary of Agriculture), *The Western Range,* Washington, D. C., 1936.

Paonia Fruit, Board of Trade of the North Fork Valley, Denver, 1904.

VI. *PERIODICALS AND NEWSPAPERS*

Craig, A. L. (editor), *The Paonian,* July 15, 1937.

Craig, A. L. (editor), "Somerset Mine," *The Paonian,* September 7, 1936.

Craig, A. L. (editor), "Tede Hice—Hunter," *The Paonian,* October, 1934.

Coburn, W. S., History of the Fruit Industry," *The North Fork Times,* May 21, 1897.

Ferguson, Olivia Spalding, "Early History of Delta County," *The Delta County Tribune,* October 20, 1932.

Johnston, A. C. (editor), "Tede Hice—Cow-puncher," *Denver Daily Record Stockman,* 1934.

Lossius, Rudolph (editor), "North Fork Canals," *The North Fork Times,* October 1, 1897.

Lossius, Rudolph (editor), "The North Fork Valley and its Citizens," *The North Fork Times,* August, 1899.

Lossius, Rudolph (editor), "Maher and Crawford," *The North Fork Times,* October 1, 1897.

Lossius, Rudolph (editor), "History of North Fork Valley and its Prominent Citizens," *The North Fork Times,* October 1, 1897.

Price, Adah, "Early History of Delta County," *The Delta Independent,* September, 1921.

Russel, Howard (editor), "Description of Delta County," *Delta Independent,* December 31, 1896.

Thomas, Alfred Barnaby, "Spanish Expeditions into Colorado," *The Colorado Magazine,* Volume 1, November 1924.

Wilson, Paul, "The North Fork Valley," *Rocky Mountain Resources,* Colorado Springs, Colorado, December, 1907.

Yauger, G. S., "Irrigation in the North Fork," *The Irrigation Era,* published in Denver, Colorado, November, 1898.

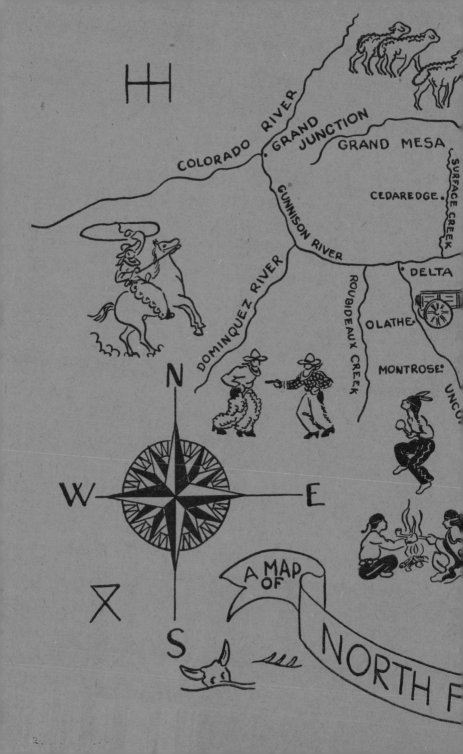

Taming an Outlaw
—Courtesy H. H. Garnett.

Article 15. The United States hereby agree to furnish the Indians the teachers, carpenters, millers, farmers and blacksmiths, as herein contemplated, and that such appropriations shall be made from time to time, on the estimates of the Secretary of the Interior, as will be sufficient to employ such persons.

Article 16. No treaty for the cession of any portion or part of the reservation herein described, which may be held in common, shall be of any validity or force as against the said Indians, unless executed and signed by at least three-fourths of all the adult male Indians occupying or interested in the same; and no cession by the tribe shall be understood or construed in such manner as to deprive, without his consent, any individual member of the tribe of his right to any tract of land selected by him, as provided in article 7 of this treaty.

Article 17. All appropriations now made, or to be hereafter made, as well as goods and stock due these Indians under existing treaties, shall apply as if this treaty had not been made, and be divided proportionately among the seven bands named in this treaty, as also shall all annuities and allowances hereafter to be made; provided, that if any chief of either of the confederated bands make war against the people of the United States or in any manner violate this treaty in any essential part, said chief shall forfeit his position as chief and all rights to any of the benefits of this treaty; but further provided, any Indian of any of these confederated bands who shall remain at peace and abide by the terms of this treaty in all its essentials shall be entitled to its benefits and provisions, notwithstanding his particular chief and band may have forfeited their rights thereto.

TREATY NEGOTIATED WITH THE UTES[1] 1873

ARTICLES of convention, made and entered into at the Los Pinos agency for the Ute Indians, on the 13th day of September, 1873, by and between Felix R. Brunot, commissioner in behalf of the United States, and the chiefs, head men and men of the Uncompahgre, Tabequache, Mouache, Capote, Weeminuche, Yampa, Grand River and Uintah bands of Ute Indians, witnesseth:

[1] *Senate Documents,* Volume I, p. 151.

needed for the Uintah, Yampa and Grand River agency, known as the White River agency.

Article 10. At any time after ten years from the making of this treaty, the United States shall have the privilege of withdrawing the farmers, blacksmiths, carpenters and millers herein, and in the treaty of October 7th, 1863, referred to in article 1 of this treaty, provided for, but in case of such withdrawal, an additional sum thereafter of ten thousand dollars per annum shall be devoted to the education of said Indians, and the Commissioner of Indian Affairs shall, upon careful inquiry into their condition, make such rules and regulations, subject to the approval of the Secretary of the Interior, for the expenditure of said sum as will best promote the educational and moral improvement of said Indians.

Article 11. That a sum, sufficient in the discretion of Congress, for the absolute wants of said Indians, but not to exceed thirty thousand dollars per annum, for thirty years, shall be expended, under the direction of the Secretary of the Interior, for clothing, blankets and such other articles of utility as he may think proper and necessary upon full official reports of the condition and wants of said Indians.

Article 12. That an additional sum, sufficient in the discretion of Congress (but not to exceed thirty thousand dollars per annum), to supply the wants of said Indians for food, shall be annually expended under the direction of the Secretary of the Interior, in supplying said Indians with beef, mutton, wheat, flour, beans and potatoes, until such time as said Indians shall be found to be capable of sustaining themselves.

Article 13. That for the purpose of inducing said Indians to adopt habits of civilized life and become self-sustaining, the sum of forty-five thousand dollars, for the first year, shall be expended, under the direction of the Secretary of the Interior, in providing each lodge or head of a family in said confederated bands with one gentle American cow, as distinguished from the ordinary or Mexican or Texas breed, and five head of sheep.

Article 14. The said confederated bands agree that whensoever, in the opinion of the President of the United States, the public interest may require it, that all roads, highways and railroads, authorized by law, shall have the right of way through the reservations herein designated.